P9-DUG-646

STRESS-FREE SAT®

A Step-by-Step Beginner's Guide to SAT Preparation

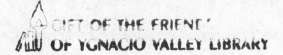
The Staff of The Princeton Review

PrincetonReview.com

Penguin
Random
House

The Princeton Review
110 East 42nd Street, 7th Floor
New York, NY 10017

Published in the United States by Penguin Random House LLC, New York, and in Canada by Random House of Canada, a division of Penguin Random House Ltd., Toronto.

Terms of Service: The Princeton Review Online Companion Tools ("Student Tools") for retail books are available for only the two most recent editions of that book. Student Tools may be activated only once per eligible book purchased for a total of 24 months of access. Activation of Student Tools more than once per book is in direct violation of these Terms of Service and may result in discontinuation of access to Student Tools Services.

ISBN: 978-0-525-57152-0
eBook ISBN: 978-0-525-57190-2
ISSN: 2766-9548

SAT® is a trademark registered by the College Board, which is not affiliated with, and does not endorse, this product.

The Princeton Review is not affiliated with Princeton University.

Permission has been granted to reprint portions of the following:

"Why Are Blue Whales So Gigantic?" by Eric M. Keen. Reproduced with permission. Copyright © 2020 SCIENTIFIC AMERICAN, a Division of Springer Nature America, Inc. All rights reserved.

Ed Yong, "Empathic rats spring each other from jail." © 2011 by Ed Yong.

3D printers: A revolutionary frontier for medicine." ©2017 by Ivar Mendez. Originally published at theconversation.com.Republished through Creative Commons License

EDITORIAL

Rob Franek, Editor-in-Chief
David Soto, Director of Content Development
Stephen Koch, Student Survey Manager
Deborah Weber, Director of Production
Gabriel Berlin, Production Design Manager
Selena Coppock, Director of Editorial
Aaron Riccio, Senior Editor
Meave Shelton, Senior Editor
Chris Chimera, Editor
Anna Goodlett, Editor
Eleanor Green, Editor
Orion McBean, Editor
Patricia Murphy, Editorial Assistant

RANDOM HOUSE PUBLISHING TEAM

Tom Russell, VP, Publisher
Alison Stoltzfus, Publishing Director
Brett Wright, Senior Editor
Amanda Yee, Associate Managing Editor
Ellen Reed, Production Manager
Suzanne Lee, Designer
Eugenia Lo, Publishing Assistant

For customer service, please contact **editorialsupport@review.com,** and be sure to include:

- full title of the book
- ISBN
- page number

Editor: Chris Chimera
Production Editors: Liz Dacey and Emma Parker
Production Artist: Jennifer Chapman

Printed in the United States of America.

10 9 8 7 6 5 4 3 2 1

Acknowledgments

Special thanks to Sara Kuperstein, Amy Minster, and Cynthia Ward for their expert review and contributions to the content of this book.

Thanks also to Anne Bader, Kevin Baldwin, Gabby Budzon, Nicole Cosme, Anne Goldberg-Baldwin, Brad Kelly, Spencer LeDoux, Jomil London, Dave MacKenzie, Scott O'Neal, Danielle Perrini, Benjamin Tallon, Jess Thomas, and Jimmy Williams for their contributions to this book.

The Princeton Review would also like to thank Jennifer Chapman, Liz Dacey, and Emma Parker for their time and attention to each page.

Special thanks to Adam Robinson, who conceived of and perfected the Joe Bloggs approach to standardized tests, and many other techniques in this book.

Contents

Get More (Free) Content.. vi

Introduction... 1

STEP 1: Research Schools **5**

STEP 2: Take a Practice Test **19**

Mini Practice Test.. 21

Mini Practice Test: Answers and Explanations.............................. 61

STEP 3: Determine Your Goals **91**

STEP 4: Make Your Goals Specific **97**

STEP 5: Make a Plan **103**

STEP 6: Learn Big Picture Strategies **117**

STEP 7: Learn Section-Specific Strategies **125**

SAT Reading.. 127

SAT Writing and Language 155

SAT Math 167

STEP 8: Next Steps **187**

Get More **(Free)** Content
at **PrincetonReview.com/prep**

As easy as **1·2·3**

1 Go to PrincetonReview.com/prep
or scan the QR code and enter the
following ISBN for your book:
9780525571520

2 Answer a few simple questions to set up
an exclusive Princeton Review account.
*(If you already have one, you can
just log in.)*

3 Enjoy access to
your **FREE** content!

Once you've registered, you can...

- Get our take on any recent or pending updates to the SAT

- Take a full-length practice PSAT, SAT, and/or ACT

- Get valuable advice about the college application process, including tips for writing a great essay and where to apply for financial aid

- If you're still choosing between colleges, use our searchable rankings of *The Best 386 Colleges* to find out more information about your dream school.

Need to report a potential **content** issue?

Contact **EditorialSupport@review.com** and include:

- full title of the book
- ISBN
- page number

Need to report a **technical** issue?

Contact **TPRStudentTech@review.com** and provide:

- your full name
- email address used to register the book
- full book title and ISBN
- Operating system (Mac/PC) and browser (Firefox, Safari, etc.)

INTRODUCTION

What is the SAT? Do I need to take it? How do I sign up? How long is the test? WHAT AM I GOING TO DO???

If the above freak-out sounds familiar, relax! We're here to help. You probably have a lot of questions about the SAT, most or all of which will be answered in this book. The SAT can be an intimidating test, and there's a lot to know about it, but let's take it one step at a time. This book will help you break your SAT prep into 8 easy-to-manage steps and put it into the context of your own personal college application journey. Let's start with the most basic question:

Do I need to take the SAT, and what is it for?

The SAT and the ACT are two different tests that are used for admission to colleges and universities in the United States (and some schools internationally). The SAT is made by a company called the College Board. These days, any school that requires a standardized test will allow you to take either the SAT or the ACT, so which one you take comes down to your preference. Since you've picked up this book, we'll assume that you have chosen the SAT. That being said, if you take a practice test and find you really hate the SAT, consider trying a practice ACT to see whether you like the ACT any better.

Not all schools require you to take the SAT or ACT, but enough of them do that if you are planning to apply to college, you will most likely need to take one of them. Even when schools do not require one of these tests, a great SAT score can still help you get in and earn scholarships.

> If you decide to switch to the ACT, check out *Stress-Free ACT* or *ACT Prep*.

What does the SAT mean for me?

An SAT score in and of itself is meaningless. It isn't an indication of your intelligence, your worth as a human being, or even your academic skills. If you don't score as high as you'd like on the SAT, it does not mean that you aren't smart or capable. The SAT tests one thing: your ability to take the SAT. If you are very good at the skills that are tested on the SAT, then you will do very well on the SAT. If you haven't yet mastered the SAT skills, you may have trouble with the test, even if you have great academic skills. Let's take a look at some of the differences:

Tested on the SAT	Not Tested on the SAT
Choosing the correct answer out of 4 options	Your intelligence, creativity, passion, attitude, and self-worth
Answering questions in a short amount of time	How well you will do, academically, in college
Answering questions about a reading passage	How much effort you put into your schoolwork
Knowing a handful of grammar and punctuation rules	The depth of your understanding of various topics and your ability to explain yourself on those topics
Using a little of the math you've learning in school, and maybe some you haven't	Your abilities in subjects that don't appear on the SAT
Your ability to read carefully and to avoid tricks and traps	Most of what you've learned in school about reading, math, and writing

When you look at what is tested on the SAT, are those the same things you learned in school? Unless you went to SAT school (then why are you reading this book?), the answer is "NO!" That's why you shouldn't compare the SAT to how well you do in school. You've learned much more in school than what is tested on the SAT, and some of the skills you need for the SAT simply aren't taught in school at all.

So, what's a student to do? Learn the skills you need for the SAT. It all starts with a change to your mindset. We aren't going to teach you everything there is to know about literature, writing, and math. To get a great SAT score, you only need to master the topics that actually appear on the test and the strategies needed to approach them.

What is a great SAT score?

Well, it all depends on where you plan to apply to college. A great score at one school might not be a great score at another school. There is no such thing as a "passing" score on the SAT, but there is such thing as an "average" score. Every college has an average SAT score, and you can use that score to figure out how your own SAT score compares. We'll go into the SAT structure and scoring in Step 3. For now, just keep in mind that the SAT is scored from 400–1600, and that main score is the sum of two 800-point scoring areas. For reference, the national average SAT score is about 1050.

That leads us to the next topic. Before you do anything else with the SAT, you need to research colleges! Just like we said above, you'll need to compare your starting SAT score with the score you need for the schools you personally plan to apply to. So, how do you figure out what score you need? Read on to find out!

STEP 1: Research Schools

Throughout your SAT prep, remember your ultimate goal: get admitted into the college *of your choice*. Every student needs a target score to aim for, but it's impossible to know what you are aiming for until you find out what score you need for the schools you plan to apply to.

Let's start by understanding why people go to college. There are several different degrees you can earn at a college or university. The first type of degree, after a high school diploma, is an **Associate's degree**, which typically takes two years of full-time study to earn, often at a community college or technical school. Some jobs that often require only an Associate's degree are physical therapist assistant, dental hygienist, paralegal, and veterinary technician. The next type of degree is a four-year **Bachelor's degree**. This is what is most often referred to as a "college diploma." You don't need to earn an Associate's degree first in order to earn a Bachelor's degree, although some four-year programs will award you one after the first two years. After earning a Bachelor's degree, you may choose to attend graduate school if you are pursuing a career that requires an advanced degree, such as a **Master's degree** or a **Ph.D**.

Now that we've talked about the types of degrees you can earn, let's take a look at some of the different types of higher education institutions.

Community College/Junior College

These schools are generally open to everyone. They are often the least expensive college option, especially if you're local. Some offer Bachelor's degrees, and all offer Associate's degrees. You don't need an SAT or ACT score to get in, but your standardized test score can help with placement into higher-level courses.

College

In the United States, the word "college" is commonly used for just about any level of study after high school. When "College" is part of the name of a school, though, it generally means that the school is smaller, has more limited courses, and offers Bachelor's degrees but not many graduate degrees. A liberal arts college allows or requires students to study a wide variety of subjects, not just one. Most colleges require SAT or ACT scores.

Technical/Trade/Vocational School

These schools are designed to get you a job in a certain field. Typically, students earn a certificate in a trade (such as cosmetology or emergency medical response) instead of a degree. Programs focus students' time on the skills they need for a future career in their chosen trade. Like community colleges, most are open enrollment, so test scores generally aren't required.

University

A university is typically a larger school, and it may contain multiple colleges (such as the College of Engineering or the College of Medicine). Universities typically offer graduate programs in addition to Bachelor's, and sometimes Associate's, degrees. These schools offer the broadest range of classes and generally require SAT or ACT scores.

As you can see, if you want to go to trade school or a community college, you can stop here because you won't need to worry about the SAT. If you plan to apply to a four-year college or university, however, let's take a look at how to research which ones to apply to.

One great way to save money is to attend a local community or junior college for two years and take the general required courses such as English and Math. Then, transfer to a college or university for classes in your desired major to earn your Bachelor's Degree. Speak with a counselor first to ensure that your credits will transfer.

Public? Private? For-profit?

Public colleges and universities are partially funded by states, so they tend to be less expensive, especially if you live in that state. Private schools are more expensive but may offer more services to students, and their costs typically don't vary based on where you are from. For-profit institutions are run like businesses. This does not necessarily mean they can't provide a quality education, but not all are accredited, which means they may not be able to offer you a real degree for your money. Check to make sure any institution you're interested in is accredited to offer the degree you're seeking.

Start by considering what you are looking for in a college. For instance, do you want to attend a school near where you currently live or in a different state or region? What career do you hope to pursue, and what kind of degree is required? How much can you afford to pay for college?

You may have an idea about some things you are looking for and not others. That's okay! For example, it's completely fine if you're not sure yet what you would like to study in college. Here are a few ways to find information about schools that might be a good fit:

- Both the Princeton Review (https://www.princetonreview.com/college-search) and the College Board (https://bigfuture.collegeboard.org/college-search) have College Search tools on their websites that allow you to choose the criteria you're looking for. Then you'll be shown profiles of schools that match your preferences.

- *The Best 386 Colleges* is a Princeton Review book with college profiles and rankings by category, including quotes from actual students.

- Talk to a college counselor. If your school has guidance counselors, schedule a meeting to discuss schools that might be a good fit for you. You can also find a private college counselor.

Need a College Admissions Counselor?
The Princeton Review has counselors available. For more information, go to https://www.princetonreview.com/college-admissions/college-counseling

What's the best college?

You will often see lists that claim to broadly rank colleges against each other, but these lists don't mean much. Every college has its pros and cons. Generally, the colleges that are considered to be the strongest academically naturally tend to be the most selective schools (those that accept the lowest percentage of applicants). However, you should never compare one school to another based on an arbitrary ranking. One school could be superior in one program, while another could have a different program that is stronger. Above all, what matters is whether the school is a good fit for you. The fact that someone might tell you, "This is the best school!" does NOT mean it is the best school for you. For instance, if you hate sports, a school where most students love to participate in athletic events is probably not going to be the best fit, no matter how great its academics are. Likewise, if you are hoping to join a fraternity or sorority, a school that doesn't offer those organizations isn't for you.

Check out our book *Best 386 Colleges* to see college profiles to help you find the best fit.

What should I look for when I view college profiles?

Start to think about your personality and learning style as well as what you hope to do while in college. Here are just some considerations:

- What programs does the school offer?

- Where is it located, and what is the town or city like?

- How much does it cost? How much financial aid is offered?

- What do students do for fun—sports, Greek life, arts events, parties, student organizations?

- Do students live on campus, or do most commute?

- How big is the school? How big are classes?

- What is the typical student like? Would I fit in?

If you like what you see from the college profile, there are lots of ways to get more information. Here are a few:

- Look at the information provided on the school's website.

- Request a brochure or other information to be sent to you through the mail.

- Check out the school's social media pages.

- Read blogs or forums written by students.

- Reach out to someone you may know who attends the school.

- Check the admissions office's website for events near you.

- Schedule a campus visit.

Should I visit campus, and if so, what should I look for?

You may be surprised to hear that visiting campus isn't just about seeing what the buildings look like. After all, you can get that from a brochure! If possible, it's best to visit when school is in session rather than during spring or summer break. This will give you a better idea of what the campus is actually like for students.

During your visit, try to determine how you would fit in on campus. In addition to doing a tour, if the college offers overnights with students or opportunities to sit in on classes, those are great ways to get a sense of what the students are like and how the school fits with your preferences. Are students socializing and having fun, or are they keeping to themselves? Do they seem passionate about academics, or are they more focused on extracurricular activities? Try to get a feel for the campus community, since that is what you'll be surrounded by as a student. A campus visit can also be a good opportunity to introduce yourself to the admissions office if you are strongly interested in the school—consider signing up for an interview.

The College Application Process

We've established that SAT scores are one component of your college applications, but luckily they are far from the only thing colleges look at. Let's take a look at the typical parts of a college application.

The #1 thing you should know about applying to college is that every school is different. Unfortunately, we can't provide detailed universal advice because each school has its own admissions requirements. Use the following as a general guideline, but be sure to check the admissions website for each individual school to see what is required.

Application

It might seem obvious, but all colleges have some sort of application you need to fill out with information such as your name, address, high school, parent and sibling information, and extracurricular activities. Many colleges these days use what's called the Common Application, which is a website that allows you to fill out your information one time and have it sent to any participating colleges you apply to. The Common App is typically available for applicants to start filling out on August 1st, so you'll have plenty of time to gather your information and work on it. Most likely, you'll want to sit down with a parent or guardian, since you'll need some information from them. For schools that don't use the Common App, the admissions website will provide information on how to access the application.

High school transcript

Your transcript is an official document from your high school that is like a report card for your entire high school career. It shows all of the classes you took and your final grade in each one. It may also include your grade point average (GPA) and class ranking. Generally, you will contact your school's guidance or college counselor, let that person know which colleges you are applying to, and your school will send the transcripts either electronically or by mail to the colleges. Alternatively, the school might provide a sealed transcript in an envelope for you to send yourself. Either way, you most likely won't see the actual transcript.

If you are homeschooled, go to high school outside of the United States, or attend a school without traditional classes and grades, or are in any other unusual situation, check each college's admissions website to see what it says about those special circumstances. If you can't find the information you need, just call or email the admissions office.

Essay

You have probably heard of a "college essay." The good news is that you can typically write just one essay to send to every college—it is usually not specific to each school. The essay is your opportunity to showcase your writing skills but also to show the admissions officers your personality and what is important to you. The Common App provides several different broad essay topics (such as "Describe a problem you've solved or would like to solve" or "Reflect on a time when you questioned or challenged a belief or idea"), and there is also an option to write on the topic of your choice.

Test scores

You'll have the College Board send your scores directly to colleges. If you take the SAT multiple times, you'll have the option to send the scores from all the dates or just some of them. Many colleges offer a "superscore," which means if you send scores from multiple dates, they will take your highest overall Evidence-Based Reading and Writing score and highest overall Math score to create the highest total score. Other colleges require you to send all of your scores or just those from one date of your choosing, so check each school's website for what it requires.

Some schools don't require test scores, but they'll still accept them—and great scores can boost your chances. Better yet, some schools offer significant scholarships just for certain SAT scores, which can be a great reason to spend some time working on your SAT skills. Much more on SAT scores in Step 3!

Recommendations

Most colleges require you to send 2–3 recommendations from adults who aren't related to you. Some schools also specify that a certain number of the recommendations must be from teachers. Other than teachers, you may be able to ask for a recommendation from a coach, employer, or any other adult who knows you and your abilities. Again, check each school for its process, but the person writing you a recommendation may do it through the Common App or the school's website, or they may simply write the recommendation and give it to you or your guidance counselor to send to the school.

Some of the components you see here may be recommended, but not required, by some schools. In general, it's best to include any parts of the application that are recommended, in order to give yourself the best possible chance at being admitted.

Other materials

Those are the most universal requirements, but here are a few more that may be required, recommended, or just possible to include in your application.

- Portfolio or audition if you're applying for a program in the arts

- Graded paper from a high school class—so it's worth holding on to any well-written papers

- Interview, either with the admissions office or with a graduate of the school

- Grades from the first semester of senior year. If you have a great semester, you can have your school send those grades separately if they are released after the admissions deadline.

- Supplemental essays or short-answer questions that are specific to the individual school

- Résumé—if you have one and feel it better highlights your work or volunteer experiences than the space available on the application does

Most college applications are due in January, but if you're set on one top choice, you may be able to apply Early Decision or Early Action, which usually has a November or December deadline. Some schools offer rolling admissions, which means you can apply at any time of the year.

Where Does the SAT Score Fit In?

Some schools place more importance on the SAT score than others do. In general, a large state school will be looking at your SAT score and GPA first and foremost. Smaller schools also care about those numbers, but compared to bigger schools, they typically place more of an emphasis on your essay, recommendations, and other materials that show who you are as a person. It's also worth noting that while colleges will generally focus on your overall SAT score out of 1600, some programs may have more specific requirements. For instance, if you're applying to an Engineering program, you may have to hit a minimum SAT Math score. Do your research!

Determining Your Target Score

Once you have started researching schools that might be a good fit for you, start to think about your target score. Your target score is a score that you would be happy sending to those schools. The first step is finding the average SAT score of the recently admitted freshman class for each school. Then, consider the strength of the rest of your application. If you know you have taken challenging classes, have excellent grades, and expect to have strong recommendations, you might decide that it's okay if your SAT score is a little lower than the school's average. On the other hand, if the other parts of your application aren't very strong, you might decide you need to push for an above-average SAT score to balance them out. In Steps 3 and 4, we'll talk about how to make your goals more specific. For now, make sure you have an idea of what overall score you're aiming for, and then a practice test will help you figure out how much work you need to put in.

PAYING FOR COLLEGE

How much does college cost?

We mentioned earlier that local public community colleges are typically the cheapest option: on average, they cost about $3,000 to $5,000 per year (but remember, most don't offer bachelor's degrees). Likewise, in-state public schools tend to be relatively inexpensive, as they are partially funded by their states; such schools on average charge approximately $10,000 per year in tuition. You'll pay about double that for an out-of-state public college, and private colleges cost the most, with an average annual tuition of just over $35,000 and some schools charging $50,000 or more per year. By the way, that's *not* including the cost of room and board (housing and meals), healthcare, or textbooks!

Those numbers may sound unbelievable, but it's worth recognizing that most students receive some form of financial aid. This means they aren't on the hook for the full tuition amount. In fact, schools with higher tuition rates may even have more financial aid options available because those who can afford to pay the sticker price help subsidize the costs for those who can't. To make more sense of this, let's take a look at financial aid.

What is financial aid?

Financial aid helps you pay for college, and it has nothing to do with your grades or any other merits (in the next section we'll look at how your hard work can get you money for college via scholarships). Financial aid is based on how much money your family has and how much your college charges for tuition. Your family will fill out a U.S. Department of Education form called the FAFSA (Free Application for Federal Student Aid), which will determine your family's Expected Family Contribution (EFC). This is the amount of money the government thinks your family can pay for your college in a given year, based on income, savings, and other financial information. The colleges you apply to will determine your annual cost of attendance (COA), which includes tuition, fees, and room and board if you'll be living on campus. Then, the colleges will use the difference between your EFC and COA to award financial aid. Let's take a look at an example.

Let's say your family fills out the FAFSA, and the government decides your parents can afford to pay $15,000 this year for your college. Here are the schools you get accepted to:

Local Public University (LPU), COA $12,000—You aren't awarded any financial aid, because the government thinks your parents can afford at least $12,000 this year.

Out-of-State Public University (OSPU), COA $25,000—This school may award you up to $10,000 in financial aid, because the government thinks your parents can afford only $15,000 this year, and the school costs $25,000.

Private College (PC), COA $55,000—This school may award you up to $40,000 in financial aid, as that is the difference between your EFC and the COA.

You may notice we use the word *may* above. A college or university does not have to award financial aid to you, unless it has made a commitment to meet 100% of demonstrated need. Colleges with this attribute promise to award you the full difference between your EFC and the COA. When you view college profiles, you can look to see whether each school meets 100% of demonstrated need.

Types of Financial Aid

Before you get too excited about all the money coming your way, you should know that financial aid may have stipulations. If you qualify, you'll receive an offer along with your college acceptance letter. That offer will detail how the money will be awarded to you, and it may come in any combination of grants, loans, and work-study. Let's take a look at what those are.

GRANTS

This is the best kind of financial aid—you get money toward your tuition and other expenses with no strings attached. These funds never need to be paid back—it's free money. These can come from various levels of government or from the college or university.

FEDERAL LOANS

You probably have a sense of what these are: they give you money toward college, but you'll have to pay back the loans starting six months after you graduate. There are also two key types of loans, which have to do which the way in which they accrue interest. (That is, you'll ultimately pay back more than you borrowed.) With subsidized loans, the government pays the interest on your loans until the six-month grace period ends, at which point you're now responsible for making payments. For unsubsidized loans, interest accrues while you are attending school, so you'll be starting out your payments with a larger balance than the amount you borrowed.

Clearly, subsidized loans are better, but they have a maximum limit, so some students may need to take out both types of loans. It's worth noting that subsidized loans are only available for students with demonstrated need, whereas students who don't qualify for financial aid or need to make up a gap between the cost of attendance and the amount of financial aid they receive can still take out unsubsidized loans.

FEDERAL WORK-STUDY

Work-study is a type of financial aid that you have to work for. This program qualifies you for a certain amount of money that you can earn through part-time employment, either on campus (such as in the library or dining hall) or in the community (often for a nonprofit or community organization). Of course, you can also find your own job and make money unrelated to the work-study award. However, some programs may only be available to students who qualify for Federal Work-Study, and other jobs may prioritize those students. Like any other job, you'll earn an hourly wage, and you can apply your paycheck to your tuition or simply keep the money for daily expenses.

What if...

There are a couple of big concerns you might have here. First off, what if the government decides your family can afford a certain amount, but your family can't or doesn't want to pay that amount? Or what if a college doesn't meet 100% of your demonstrated need? For instance, let's say OSPU (from page 14) offers you only $5,000 of the $10,000 gap between your EFC and the school's COA. In either of these cases, you may decide to choose a more affordable school, or you may have to come up with another way to pay for college. Perhaps you can save up money from a job before college starts—or even take a gap year to earn more before you begin school. It's also possible to take out private loans, rather than government ones, but this can be risky because private loans typically have higher interest rates and aren't as flexible when it comes to repayment.

Merit Aid

Another way to help cover the gap is by applying for and winning a scholarship. Whereas financial aid doesn't take into consideration your grades or any personal attributes—it's only related to how much you have the ability to pay—scholarships do. There are many sources of scholarships, and they generally relate to your merit, which could include your grades, test scores, community involvement, leadership, and other areas of excellence, such as athletics. And while some scholarships may take your financial need into account, some don't. For instance, in our example from earlier, even though you don't qualify for financial aid from LPU, that school could still offer you a scholarship if the admissions officers really want you to attend because of all of your great attributes.

You may receive a scholarship from a college you have been accepted to, or you may apply for a scholarship from an outside organization. You may also have to meet certain criteria for a scholarship, such as living in a certain region, having a certain ethnic background, or pursuing a career in a particular field. To apply for a scholarship, you will typically have to fill out an application, and some scholarships require you to write an essay or complete a project such as a video. A scholarship could be as low as $50 (every little bit helps!) or as high as what's commonly called a full ride (your entire tuition along with room and board). Some scholarships give you money only once, while others are for all four years—assuming you continue to meet the conditions of the scholarship.

HOW DO I FIND OUT ABOUT SCHOLARSHIPS?

In the admissions process, you'll either automatically qualify based on a school's preset criteria or be manually selected for a scholarship if the school wants to offer you an additional incentive to attend. When you're researching colleges, you should be able to find information about scholarships on each school's website. For instance, some schools automatically offer scholarships based on an applicant's SAT or ACT scores and/or GPA (the average of your grades from high school). It's worth looking into that because a few months of test prep could pay off big time in the form of a significant reduction to your college costs. The PSAT in 11th grade can also qualify you for a National Merit Scholarship if you score in the top 1% of students in your state.

For outside scholarships, start by asking your high school guidance counselor. Your counselor may be aware of local scholarships that you may be eligible for. You can also find websites with lists of thousands of different scholarships, and you can filter them to find the ones you qualify for. You can apply for as many scholarships as you want. Just remember that there are many other students applying for them, so you may be best off focusing your time on the scholarships for which you feel your background makes you especially well suited.

When you get your acceptance letters and financial aid offers, really consider what makes the most financial sense. Working hard in college and taking advantage of every opportunity that's available to you will often do far more to set you up for future success than name recognition.

A Few Words of Advice

Be careful not to mortgage your future on your present-day desires. Think about how much debt each offer on the table would leave you with, and measure that against how much you're likely to be making from your chosen career. On average, college graduates make about $50,000 a year and owe about $30,000, and with interest, that can take a considerable amount of time pay off, especially if you also have to pay for rent and other necessities. (This also assumes you'll immediately land a job.) There are millions of successful people who graduated from state universities and other non-brand-name schools, so finding an affordable good-fit school may be more prudent than attending one that will leave you drowning in debt.

STEP 2: Take a Practice Test

Now that you have some idea of where you may want to apply for college and what kind of SAT score you will need, it's time to get more familiar with the SAT. Namely, it's time to find out what your starting score is: the score that you'd get if you took the SAT right now. Knowing your starting score will help you figure out how much work you need to put in to achieve the score you need when you take the official SAT. You might find that you are already scoring within the range that you need and you don't need to prep at all. On the other hand, you might find that you will need to put in a fair amount of effort to achieve the score you need. Either way, it is extremely helpful to know your starting score.

In this chapter, you will find a sample of each type of content you can expect to see on the SAT. If you have not yet taken a full practice SAT, you can try out these sample passages and questions to get a sense of what topics are tested and how comfortable you are with them. Alternatively, Steps 6 and 7 of this book provide you with some great SAT strategies, so you may also choose not to try the sample passages and questions until after you have learned our strategies. The choice is yours!

Regardless of whether you try the samples now or later, it's a good idea to take a full-length practice test now. It's the only way to determine your starting score. You can find a free practice test on the official SAT website, www.collegeboard.org/sat. If you want to save printer ink, check with your guidance counselor's office to see whether a paper practice test is available there. Alternatively, if you register this book online following the instructions under "Get More (Free) Content" on page vi, you can access our free SAT practice test.

Sometimes students feel intimidated to take a practice test or feel they need to do some preparation first. Keep in mind that a practice test is just that—practice. There are no stakes whatsoever. No one will ever see your practice test score, and if you bomb it, who cares? It's also not necessary to prep before taking your first practice SAT. When you take the practice test, you will find out the question types and topics that were easy for you, as well as those that were hard for you. If you know what aspects of the test you find easy or hard, you can focus your time around your *own* strengths and weaknesses and maximize your ability to get the score you need. If you prep before determining what those easy and hard things are, you might not use your time as efficiently. Steps 4 and 5 of this book will help you determine how best to prep based on your practice test scores.

You can check out the following sample content to get an idea of what the SAT tests. However, you should take a full-length practice test before moving on to Steps 3 through 5 to get the most out of this book.

Mini Practice Test

The following sample questions are set up like a real SAT test. The sections are reflective of the type of content you will see on the test but with fewer questions. To help you get familiar with each section, we've included the actual instructions you will see on test day. Make sure to read them now so you don't have to waste time when taking the real test.

You may notice that the practice questions found here, particularly the math sections, are not always numbered sequentially. We've done this to indicate where a given question may show up on the actual exam and thus help you anticipate where a certain topic may be tested and how.

Reading Test

DIRECTIONS

Each passage or pair of passages below is followed by a number of questions. After reading each passage or pair, choose the best answer to each question based on what is stated or implied in the passage or passages and in any accompanying graphics (such as a table or graph).

Questions 21–31 are based on the following passage and supplementary material.

This passage is adapted from Ed Yong, "Empathic rats spring each other from jail." ©2011 by Ed Yong. Figures from Empathy and Pro-Social Behavior in Rats by Inbal Ben-Ami Bartal, Jean Decety, Peggy Mason. Reprinted with permission from AAAS.

You enter a room with two cages. One contains a friend, who is clearly distressed. The other contains a bar of chocolate, which clearly
Line isn't. What do you do? While a few people would
5 probably go for the chocolate first (and you know who you are), most would choose to free the friend. And so, it seems, would a rat. Inbal Ben-Ami Bartal from the University of Chicago found that rats will quickly learn to free a trapped cage-
10 mate, even when they get nothing in return, or when there's a tasty chocolate distraction around. Bartal thinks that the rats conduct their prison breaks because they empathise with one another.
Past studies have shown that rats are sensitive
15 to each other's emotions, 'catching' them from one another. But Bartal wanted to know if this "emotional contagion" would actually motivate

rats to help one another. Would empathy lead to action? She kept her rats in pairs for two weeks,
20 and then placed one of them in a cage. The trapped rats were clearly stressed – Bartal used a bat detector to show that they were occasionally making high-pitched alarm calls. Their partners could free them by pushing against a restraining
25 door and tipping it over. That's what they did, although most took a week to learn how.
Bartal found that the rats spent more time exploring the cage, and were more likely to open it, when there was another rat inside. It didn't
30 matter if the liberated rat got nothing in return. Even when the rats were faced with a second cage containing delicious chocolate chips, they freed their cage-mate as often as they went for the food. They even shared their chocolate bounty with
35 their liberated pals. "Empathy is a truly powerful motivator, on a par with the desire for chocolates!" says Frans de Waal, who studies how animals think.
Stephanie Preston, who works on animal
40 emotions, says that Bartal has strengthened the case made by previous studies. "As shown

CONTINUE ➤

previously, the rodents were not only empathically
aroused by the emotion of [another rat], they
took direct action to help. This is the definition

45 of empathy," she says. There are alternative
explanations, but none of them are strong. They
weren't just trying to silence the grating alarm
calls from their trapped peers, because such calls
were too rare to be a potent motivator. They

50 weren't just curious about the trapped rat, because
they still opened the cages if they were very
familiar with the animal inside. And they weren't
just looking for something to do, for the door
mechanism was difficult. The only explanation

55 that really fits the rodents' actions is that they were
trying to end the distress of the trapped rat, or
perhaps their own distress at seeing their cage-
mate's plight.

   "The study is truly ground-breaking," adds
60 de Waal. It shows that rodents are not just
affected by the emotions of others, but that
empathy motivates altruism. De Waal suggests
that the rats' behaviour is the result of ancient
neural circuits that allow mammals to "make the

65 situation of others their own to some degree, thus
offering them an emotional stake in it." These
circuits underlie the behaviour of apes, dolphins,
elephants, rats, and probably more. De Waal
thinks that they originated from the care that

70 mammal mothers offered towards their young,
which might explain why female rats (like female
chimps and female humans) seem to be more
empathic than male ones. In Bartal's experiment,
all the female rats opened doors for a trapped

75 individual, compared to just three-quarters of the
males.

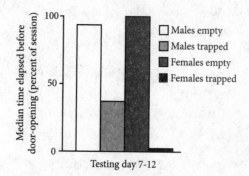

Figure 1
Median Time Before Cage
Opening

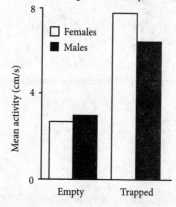

Figure 2
Average Movement Speed

The graphs above show the reactions of rats in four
cases: males reacting to an empty cage, females reacting
to an empty cage, males reacting to a cage with a
trapped mate, and females reacting to a cage with a
trapped mate.

CONTINUE ▶

21

In line 17, Bartal uses the phrase "emotional contagion" to suggest that emotions can

A) correct mood disorders in mammals.

B) shorten the time in which rats learn to open gates.

C) cause an apathetic reaction among test subjects.

D) spread in an empathic way between rats.

22

While discussing the design of the experiment, the author indicates that the rats were "stressed" (line 21) because they

A) were placed in a restrained environment.

B) faced a difficult learning task.

C) were responding to the emotional distress of their cage-mates.

D) had been paired with an unfamiliar cage-mate.

23

Which choice provides the best evidence for the conclusion that rats are motivated by factors other than empathy?

A) Lines 23-26 ("Their . . . how")

B) Lines 31-33 ("Even . . . food")

C) Lines 54-58 ("The only . . . plight")

D) Lines 62-66 ("De Waal . . . it")

24

Which finding, if accurate, would undermine Bartal's results?

A) Mammals that engage in less maternal care for offspring are shown to be less empathic in experimental settings than are those who offer more care.

B) Rats that had previously been trapped showed a high level of empathy when faced with the task of freeing the cage-mate that had originally freed them.

C) Other species of rodents are found to show different levels of empathic response to their cage-mates when placed in an environment that mimics Bartal's experiment.

D) A trial with a similar design showed that rats opened a cage containing cheese more often than they opened a cage containing their cage-mate.

CONTINUE ➤

25

As used in line 67, "underlie" most nearly means

A) influence.

B) hide.

C) prove.

D) alter.

26

It can most reasonably be inferred that Bartal's study supports which of the following statements about mammals?

A) Some mammals make stronger displays of empathy than rats do.

B) Some empathic behaviors found in most mammals are not found in rats.

C) Some female mammals exhibit observable empathic behavior more often than male mammals do.

D) Some stressful conditions may be prevented for mammals involved in studies.

27

Which choice provides the best evidence for the answer to the previous question?

A) Lines 39-41 ("Stephanie . . . studies")

B) Lines 45-46 ("There . . . strong")

C) Lines 66-68 ("These . . . more")

D) Lines 73-76 ("In Bartal's . . . males")

28

The last paragraph mainly serves to

A) compare this study to previous studies, in which researchers found no evidence of empathy in rats.

B) suggest an explanation for the results of the study.

C) explain the role of long-existing brain pathways in mammals other than rats.

D) present a conclusion that challenges an existing scientific viewpoint.

29

According to figure 1, on average, males reacting to a trapped mate opened the door after what percent of the session had occurred?

A) Between 10 and 20 percent

B) Between 30 and 40 percent

C) Between 65 and 75 percent

D) Between 90 and 100 percent

CONTINUE ▶

30

Which conclusion about the mean activity of the rats is best supported by figure 2?

A) The contents of the cage had a greater effect on mean activity level than did the rat's sex.

B) The rats encountering cages that contained a mate had lower activity levels than did rats encountering empty cages.

C) The rat's sex was a significantly better indicator of mean activity level than were the contents of the cage.

D) The mean activity level of male rats greatly exceeded the mean activity level of female rats.

31

The data presented in figures 1 and 2 best support the conclusion that compared with rats reacting to a cage containing a trapped mate, rats reacting to an empty cage were more likely to

A) have a lower activity level and display more distress over denial of food.

B) open the cage sooner and have a lower activity level.

C) open the cage later and display more empathic behavior.

D) open the cage later and have a lower activity level.

CONTINUE

Questions 32–42 are based on the following passage.

This passage is adapted from a speech given by Lucy Stone in 1848 at the Women's Rights Convention at Seneca Falls, New York.

In education, in marriage, in religion, in everything, disappointment is the lot of woman. It shall be the business of my life to deepen this
Line disappointment in every woman's heart until
5   she bows down to it no longer. The question of Woman's Rights is a practical one. The notion has prevailed that it was only an ephemeral idea; that it was but women claiming the right to smoke cigars in the streets, and to frequent bar
10   rooms. Others have supposed it a question of comparative intellect; others still, of sphere. Too much has already been said and written about woman's sphere. Trace all the doctrines to their source and they will be found to have no basis
15   except in the usages and prejudices of the age. This is seen in the fact that what is tolerated in woman in one country is not tolerated in another. Wendell Phillips says, "The best and greatest thing one is capable of doing, that is his sphere." I have
20   confidence in the Father to believe that when He gives us the capacity to do anything. He does not make a blunder. Leave women, then, to find their sphere. And do not tell us before we are born even, that our province is to cook dinners, darn
25   stockings, and sew on buttons.

We are told woman has all the rights she wants; and even women, I am ashamed to say, tell us so. They mistake the politeness of men for rights—seats while men stand in this hall

30   tonight, and their adulations; but these are mere courtesies. We want rights. The flour merchant, the house builder, and the postman charge us no less on account of our sex; but when we endeavor to earn money to pay all these, then,
35   indeed, we find the difference. Man, if he have energy, may hew out for himself a path where no mortal has ever trod, held back by nothing but what is in himself; the world is all before him, where to choose; and we are glad for you,
40   brothers, men, that is so. But the same society that drives forth the young man, keeps woman at home—a dependent—working little cats on worsted, and little dogs on punctured paper; but if she goes heartily and bravely to give herself to
45   some worthy purpose, she is out of her sphere and she loses caste. Women working in tailor shops are paid one-third as much as men. Someone in Philadelphia has stated that women make fine shirts for twelve and a half cents apiece; that no
50   woman can make more than nine a week, and the sum thus earned, after deducting rent, fuel, etc., leaves her just three and a half cents a day for bread. Female teachers in New York are paid fifty dollars a year, and for every such situation
55   there are five hundred applications. I know not what you believe of God, but I believe He gave yearnings and longings to be filled, and that He did not mean all our time should be devoted to feeding and clothing the body.
60   The present condition of woman causes a horrible perversion of the marriage relation. It is asked of a lady, "Has she married well?" "Oh, yes, her husband is rich." Woman must marry for a

CONTINUE ➤

home, and you men are the sufferers by this; for a
65 woman who loathes you may marry you because
you have the means to get money which she can
not have. But when woman can enter the lists with
you and make money for herself, she will marry
you only for deep and earnest affection.
70   I am detaining you too long, many of you
standing, that I ought to apologize, but women
have been wronged so long that I may wrong you
a little....I have seen a woman at manual labor
turning out chair-legs in a cabinetshop, with a
75 dress short enough not to drag in the shavings.
I wish other women would imitate her in this. It
made her hands harder and broader, it is true, but
I think a hand with a dollar and a quarter a day in
it, better than one with a crossed ninepence.... The
80 widening of woman's sphere is to improve her lot.
Let us do it, and if the world scoff, let it scoff—if it
sneer, let it sneer.

Stone's main purpose in the passage is to

A) argue that women should be free to choose
their employment and be fairly compensated.

B) claim that women should strive to embrace a
more male-centric societal sphere.

C) assert that women should be allowed to
participate in the same recreational activities
as men.

D) demonstrate that more women should
be proactive in pursuing employment
opportunities typically held by men.

Which statement best describes a technique used
by Stone throughout her speech to support her
central point?

A) She underscores the rationality of her beliefs
by stating that they are already held by
society.

B) She supports each assertion with a captivating
personal anecdote.

C) She criticizes society's beliefs by describing
instances in which women have been given
fair pay.

D) She presents a series of troubling conditions
and illustrates their consequences.

How does Stone develop her argument about a
limited woman's "sphere" (line 11) throughout
the passage?

A) She explains how the concept was created and
then calls upon her audience to fight against
it.

B) She claims that past definitions of the concept
are irrelevant and encourages women to
become more vocal.

C) She refutes the concept as baseless and then
illustrates its problematic impact.

D) She emphasizes that the concept is widely
accepted and then offers anecdotes in support
of preserving it.

CONTINUE ➤

35

In the passage, Stone most strongly suggests that restrictions placed on women are based on

A) the amount of respect that men demonstrate toward women.

B) perceived biological differences between men and women.

C) inevitable biases that reflect the views of men alone.

D) the beliefs and customs of a particular time and place.

36

Which choice provides the best evidence for the answer to the previous question?

A) Lines 3-5 ("It shall . . . longer")

B) Lines 13-15 ("Trace . . . age")

C) Lines 22-25 ("Leave . . . buttons")

D) Lines 35-40 ("Man . . . so")

37

In the passage, Stone draws a distinction between which of the following?

A) Superficial respect from men and equality with men

B) The work women want to do and the work they are best at

C) Employment opportunities in New York and those in Philadelphia

D) Activities preferred by men and those preferred by women

38

Which choice provides the best evidence for the answer to the previous question?

A) Lines 6-10 ("The notion . . . rooms")

B) Lines 28-31 ("They . . . courtesies")

C) Lines 40-43 ("But the . . . paper")

D) Lines 53-55 ("Female . . . applications")

CONTINUE

In context, what is the main effect of use of the word "sufferers" in line 64?

A) It highlights the harm done to men by the lack of opportunity for women.

B) It suggests that men's roles are as restrictive as women's roles.

C) It reiterates the injustice endured by women who are not well-paid for their work.

D) It suggests a global perspective on woman's rights.

According to Stone, a woman may marry a man out of a sense of affection when which goal is met?

A) A woman is able to contribute more to the financial state of her household than her husband can

B) A woman can seek employment opportunities and earn wages equally with her husband

C) A woman can ease her husband's suffering by taking on more financial responsibility

D) A woman is satisfied with the type of employment and salary that her husband has achieved

Which choice best summarizes the final paragraph?

A) Stone presents a claim and illustrates how it has been problematic throughout history.

B) Stone summarizes a problem and proposes a detailed plan to fix it.

C) Stone describes a particular example and then broadens it to support her main claim.

D) Stone describes a commonly held view and makes statements to support it.

As used in line 70, "detaining" most nearly means

A) obstructing.

B) keeping.

C) arresting.

D) hindering.

CONTINUE

Questions 43–52 are based on the following passages.

Passage 1 is adapted from Katie Feldman, "3-D-printed implants may soon fix complex injuries." 2013 by the National Science Foundation. Passage 2 is adapted from Ivar Mendez, "3D printers: A revolutionary frontier for medicine." ©2017 by Ivar Mendez. Originally published at theconversation.com.

Passage 1

In an age where 3-D printers are becoming a more and more common tool to make custom-designed objects, some researchers are using the

Line technology to manufacture replacement parts
5 for the most customized and unique object of all—the human body. With funding from the National Science Foundation, a husband and wife duo—materials scientist Susmita Bose and materials engineer Amit Bandyopadhyay—are
10 leading a team of researchers at Washington State University to create implants that more closely mimic the properties of human bone, and can be custom-designed for unusual injuries or anatomy.

Using a technology called laser engineered net
15 shaping (LENS®), these new implants integrate into the body more effectively, encouraging bone regrowth that ultimately results in a stronger, longer lasting implant. In the LENS® process, tiny particles are blown into the path of a laser and
20 melted. The material cools and hardens as soon as it is out of the laser beam, and custom parts can be quickly built up layer by layer. The process is so precise that parts can be used straight off the printer without the polishing or finishing needed
25 in traditional manufacturing.

Implant manufacturers using this strategy could simply start with a CT scan or MRI and use that to make a 3-D model of the injury. A consultation with a physician would determine
30 where the problem was and how to repair it.

The standard materials for weight-bearing implants—titanium or stainless steel—are well-tolerated by the human body. Nevertheless, these metals have different properties from the bone
35 they replace. Although bone seems stiff and solid, it in fact has some "spring" and millions of microscopic pores. Because a metal implant is much stiffer, the surrounding bone doesn't have to support as much weight as it normally would.
40 This is a significant problem with today's implants. Bones weaken and break down when they aren't properly exercised.

LENS® can be used to make parts out of many different materials, including metals and ceramics.
45 Unlike many traditional manufacturing processes, LENS® allows different kinds of materials to be easily combined into a single part. A metal core can be coated with a thin ceramic layer, for example, so that new bone is more likely to
50 grow and bond with the implant. And because LENS® builds a layer at a time, implants can be manufactured with structures that are difficult to make using traditional techniques. They can have pores in the center but be solid at the edges,
55 or have texture on the surface to help bond with bone or other biological materials.

CONTINUE ➡

Passage 2

Mission control on earth receives an urgent communication from Mars that an astronaut has fractured his shinbone. Using a handheld
60 scanning device, the crew takes images of his damaged tibia and transmits them to earth. Orthopedic surgeons then use a 3D printer to create an exact replica of the astronaut's leg from medical imaging files obtained before the voyage.
65 Surgeons on earth use a robot to stabilize the bone with a metal plate on the 3D replica. The data is transmitted back to Mars, where surgical instruments, a personalized plate and screws are 3D printed. Finally, a surgical robot operates on
70 the injured astronaut.

Though 3D printing in space is still in early development, a revolution in 3D printing is already occurring closer to home. And it has transformative implications for the future of
75 health care. Additive manufacturing, or 3D printing, uses a digital model to build an object of any size or shape—by adding successive layers of material in a single continuous run. This layering capability allows the manufacturing of complex
80 shapes, such as the intricate structure of bones or vascular channels, that would be impossible to create by other methods.

Advances in computer design and the ability to translate medical imaging—such as X-rays,
85 computerized tomography (CT), magnetic resonance imaging (MRI) or ultrasound—to digital models that can be read by 3D printers are expanding its applications in health care. 3D printing is opening a horizon of amazing
90 possibilities, such as bioprinting living tissues

with "biological ink". An advantage of 3D printing technology is that it allows for personalization of health care—customized prostheses and tailor-made drugs and organs, for example. This
95 technology may also decrease costs by disrupting supply chains and lowering the production costs of medical devices, surgical instruments and other health-care products.

Although we may be far away from surgery on
100 Mars using 3D printing technology, the advances on earth are already changing health care.

43

The author of Passage 1 suggests that an advantage of using the LENS® technique to manufacture implants is that it

A) creates parts using a process that is more efficient than that required by other manufacturing methods.

B) assesses the conditions required for successful integration of a new bone and produces those conditions in the tissues surrounding the implant.

C) can be used to help a patient regrow bones that have more spring than natural bones do.

D) enables the manufacturer to create each part out of a single material.

CONTINUE ▶

44

Which choice provides the best evidence for the answer to the previous question?

A) Lines 18-22 ("In the . . . layer")

B) Lines 22-25 ("The process . . . manufacturing")

C) Lines 35-37 ("Although . . . pores")

D) Lines 43-44 ("LENS® . . . ceramics")

45

The fourth paragraph of Passage 1 (lines 31-42) primarily serves to

A) present a hypothesis that counters real-world data presented earlier in the passage.

B) identify a natural conclusion based on information presented earlier in the passage.

C) summarize an exceptional case study that supports the author's point of view.

D) explain a problem that the technology described in the passage aims to solve.

46

As used in line 74, "implications" most nearly means

A) connotations.

B) inferences.

C) methods.

D) consequences.

47

The author of Passage 2 would most likely agree with which statement about 3D printing technology?

A) It will most likely be used in conjunction with other types of medical technology.

B) It will increase implant production costs by disrupting health-care supply chains.

C) It proves that traditional methods can still produce effective prostheses.

D) It will not result in advances in health care in the near future.

CONTINUE ➡

48

In the last sentence of Passage 2, the author uses the phrase "far away from surgery on Mars" primarily to

A) encourage governments to invest more in 3D printing for applications in space exploration.

B) recall an earlier reference in order to highlight the benefits provided by 3D printing technology.

C) contrast the uses of 3D printing technology on Mars with its uses on other planets.

D) suggest that certain applications for 3D printing technology are unrealistic.

49

Which choice best describes the relationship between Passage 1 and Passage 2?

A) Passage 1 proposes an improvement to the process detailed in Passage 2.

B) Passage 1 describes a specific example of the technology described in Passage 2.

C) Passage 1 casts doubt on the cost effectiveness of the technology described in Passage 2.

D) Passage 1 presents experimental results to support the theory discussed in Passage 2.

50

Both passages make the point that 3D printing could be useful in

A) helping scientists to determine exactly how the human body will respond to any implant.

B) preventing the natural breakdown of bones and organs over time.

C) creating unique medical devices made for a particular individual.

D) designing a novel approach to performing invasive surgeries.

51

Information in Passage 2 best supports which conclusion about the hypothetical LENS® implant discussed in Passage 1?

A) The implant would be most effective if it were based on a combination of X-ray, CT, MRI, and ultrasound imagery.

B) The shape of the implant is the key factor for successful bonding with bone.

C) The use of 3D printing technology would prevent further fracturing in the bone surrounding the implant.

D) The bone-like properties of the implant's structure could not be created using traditional methods.

CONTINUE ➡

52

Which choice provides the best evidence for the answer to the previous question?

A) Lines 57-61 ("Mission . . . earth")

B) Lines 78-82 ("This . . . methods")

C) Lines 83-88 ("Advances . . . care")

D) Lines 94-98 ("This . . . products")

STOP

If you finish before time is called, you may check your work on this section only.

Do not turn to any other section.

Writing and Language Test

DIRECTIONS

Each passage below is accompanied by a number of questions. For some questions, you will consider how the passage might be revised to improve the expression of ideas. For other questions, you will consider how the passage might be edited to correct errors in sentence structure, usage, or punctuation. A passage or a question may be accompanied by one or more graphics (such as a table or graph) that you will consider as you make revising and editing decisions.

Some questions will direct you to an underlined portion of a passage. Other questions will direct you to a location in a passage or ask you to think about the passage as a whole.

After reading each passage, choose the answer to each question that most effectively improves the quality of writing in the passage or that makes the passage conform to the conventions of standard written English. Many questions include a "NO CHANGE" option. Choose that option if you think the best choice is to leave the relevant portion of the passage as it is.

Questions 1–11 are based on the following passage.

Life Below Zero

At Earth's geographic South Pole lies the continent of Antarctica, a frigid region 5.5 million square miles in size. Its hostile interior is nearly as dry as **1** those of the Sahara Desert and features temperatures regularly below −50°F. Most species that inhabit this harsh land, including birds and fish, are concentrated in the waters and areas near the coast. **2** Similarly, while they don't exhibit much

1

A) NO CHANGE

B) that of the

C) the

D) the dryness of the

2

A) NO CHANGE

B) However,

C) Thus,

D) Moreover,

CONTINUE ➤

variety, the few creatures that do survive on the mainland of Antarctica thrive in large numbers. Their unique adaptations help 3 it to prosper in an environment that seems incompatible with what creatures need to survive.

The land in Antarctica is considered a desert because it receives so little precipitation. The water that exists there is largely ice and snow, and the frozen tundra contains very few nutrients. Although soil nutrients and water are generally considered essential for life, some of the 4 continents microbes have evolved to 5 survive. Through specially adapted genes, these organisms are able to harvest trace

3

A) NO CHANGE
B) him or her
C) one
D) them

4

A) NO CHANGE
B) continents' microbe's
C) continent's microbes'
D) continent's microbes

5

The writer is considering revising the underlined portion to the following

     survive only on air.

Should the writer make this revision here?

A) Yes, because it shows the reader the origin of the microbes in Antarctica.

B) Yes, because it clarifies the sentence's role in supporting the paragraph's main point.

C) No, because it interrupts discussion of nutrients with an unrelated detail.

D) No, because it merely restates information given earlier in the passage without relating to the paragraph's main focus.

CONTINUE

gaseous carbon monoxide, hydrogen, **6** also harvesting carbon dioxide from the air. This surprising finding indicates that hostile environments such as Antarctica can sustain microbial life that supports an ecosystem.

The continent's most prevalent land animal is a tiny worm called a nematode, which feeds on microbes. All living cells contain water, and when an organism is exposed to extremely low temperatures, the water in those cells forms sharp ice crystals that destroy the creature's body tissues. The nematode— along with other terrestrial invertebrates in **7** Antarctica uses an adaptation that allows it to survive its environment's extremely cold temperatures: the worm produces a protein in its cells that cushions the ice **8** crystals. The protein prevents them from rupturing. During winter, when all liquids are frozen, nematodes are able to **9** remove the water from their bodies and survive in a dried-out state until the summer, when they have access to water again and can come back to life.

6

A) NO CHANGE
B) and harvest
C) and
D) they also harvest

7

A) NO CHANGE
B) Antarctica,
C) Antarctica;
D) Antarctica—

8

Which choice most effectively combines the sentences at the underlined portion?

A) crystals, having to prevent
B) crystals and prevents
C) crystals, and after that, it then prevents
D) crystals, henceforth preventing

9

A) NO CHANGE
B) remove and eliminate
C) capably remove
D) eliminate to get rid of

CONTINUE

[1] During the winter, Antarctica experiences months without sunlight. [2] The summer's constant light results in little protection from sun exposure in the sparse Antarctic environment. [3] This duality presents another challenge to organisms in that they must adapt to both extremes. [4] This total darkness prevents reliance on photosynthesis for nutrition. [5] The fact that plants, animals, and microbes have adapted to thrive in a climate that provides so little of what is commonly deemed necessary for survival **10** is surprising because it contradicts what researchers had believed for hundreds of years. [6] Like Antarctica, planets such as Mars feature extreme temperatures and lack water and nutrients, so studying these creatures' adaptations can expand biologists' understanding about life in such hostile terrains. **11**

10

Which choice most effectively sets up the information in the next sentence?

A) NO CHANGE

B) demonstrates that organisms all over the world have their own environmental niches.

C) offers a precedent for scientists to evaluate the possibility of life on other planets.

D) will result in much more research into Antarctica's unique biological systems.

11

To make the paragraph most logical, sentence 4 should be placed

A) where it is now.

B) before sentence 1.

C) after sentence 1.

D) after sentence 2.

CONTINUE

Questions 12–22 are based on the following passage and supplementary material.

Housing Developments for Teachers

School districts, worried about retaining teachers but unable or unwilling to increase salaries, are looking for ways to provide **12** additional benefits that might keep teachers in their districts. In expensive cities, teachers who earn less money than people with other comparable employment opportunities are more likely to leave their jobs to seek other career positions. According to a recent study, **13** leaving the job is done by more teachers when they earn a low salary. One idea that has been gaining popularity recently is to build housing developments for teachers to live in. This proposal could help educators and provide an incentive for them to stay at their current schools. However, this potential solution does not fully address the financial reasons teachers leave their positions and the challenges in implementing teacher housing.

A reduction in housing costs could be viewed as the equivalent of a pay increase, so naturally **14** such an incentive may attract teachers. According to a study by the Learning Policy Institute, 23 percent of former teachers would consider returning to the job as a result of housing incentives. However, this factor

12

A) NO CHANGE
B) sweet perks
C) more positive aspects of the job
D) cool bonuses

13

Which choice is the most effective version of the underlined portion?

A) NO CHANGE
B) if teachers earn a low salary, more of these teachers leave their jobs.
C) more teachers leave their jobs if they earn a low salary.
D) more jobs are left by teachers when teachers earn a lower salary.

14

A) NO CHANGE
B) some
C) those
D) they

CONTINUE ▶

ranked far below salary increases and retirement benefits, among others, as a reason to return to the job. While school districts might find housing teachers to be a more economical option due to tax benefits associated with acquiring land, the teachers themselves would generally prefer to earn more locally competitive wages, which they could then spend on the housing of their choice or any number of other expenses. According to the Economic Policy Institute, teacher salaries, adjusted for inflation, have fallen since the **15** 1990s; but those of other college graduates rose by over 100 dollars per week. Housing benefits could help make teaching jobs more desirable, but they may not be enough to attract many to the job.

Current teacher housing projects **16** also have the problem of not taking into account teachers' needs. Although teacher housing has been implemented in various counties across the **17** country; housing built for teachers doesn't always go to teachers. In Los Angeles, teacher housing was built using federal subsidies (a common practice for building teacher housing), but teachers weren't able to rent any of the **18** apartments. Since the teachers' salaries were too high to qualify for low-income housing. Teacher housing that does successfully

15
A) NO CHANGE
B) 1990s, but
C) 1990s,
D) 1990s, however,

16
Which choice best introduces the paragraph?
A) NO CHANGE
B) may have a negative effect on other people seeking low-income housing.
C) also need greater oversight from community leaders.
D) may also house too few teachers to make a significant impact—or even help no teachers at all.

17
A) NO CHANGE
B) country,
C) country, and though
D) country, and

18
A) NO CHANGE
B) apartments,
C) apartments:
D) apartments; since

CONTINUE ▶

provide housing for teachers faces another problem: the number of apartments or houses available is far lower than the number of teachers in the district. For example, in Newark, NJ, a housing complex offers 204 apartments **19** and can provide housing for 2,700 teachers, not to mention those with large families who couldn't have used such housing at all. **20**

Availability of Teacher Housing

School District	Number of apartments available	Approx. number of teachers in district	Approx. number of teachers without access to teacher housing	Percentage of district teachers who could live in housing
Casa del Maestro, Santa Clara, CA	70	640	570	11%
Run Hill Ridge and Hatteras Teacher Housing, Dare County, NC	36	420	384	8.5%
Teachers Village, Newark, NJ	204	2,700	2,496	7.5%

19

Which choice provides an accurate interpretation of the chart?

A) NO CHANGE

B) and thus excludes approximately 2,496 teachers,

C) and can house all but 7.5 percent of them,

D) in a school district with around 2,496 teachers,

20

The writer is considering adding the following sentence based on information from the chart.

> On the other hand, Casa del Maestro in the Santa Clara school district leaves only 570 teachers without district-provided housing.

Should the writer make this addition here?

A) Yes, because it reinforces the argument made by supporters of teacher housing stated earlier in the paragraph.

B) Yes, because it proves how few teachers would be left without housing in Casa del Maestro compared to Teachers Village.

C) No, because it contradicts a claim about housing subsidies made earlier in the paragraph.

D) No, because it does not support the claim that teacher housing leaves out a significant number of teachers.

CONTINUE ▶

Housing for teachers does seem to be a worthwhile investment for some school districts. For example, districts in expensive cities find teacher housing appealing because employees can save time when they **21** will not need to commute long distances to work. For school districts nationwide hoping to keep teachers in their communities, however, **22** providing housing for teachers is not a universal solution.

21

A) NO CHANGE
B) did not need
C) do not need
D) could not have needed

22

Which choice provides the best conclusion to the passage?

A) NO CHANGE
B) teacher housing should be available for new teachers only.
C) houses will be more inviting than apartments.
D) studies from the Economic Policy Institute could be informative.

STOP

If you finish before time is called, you may check your work on this section only.

Do not turn to any other section.

Math Test – No Calculator

DIRECTIONS

For questions 1–15, solve each problem and choose the best answer from the choices provided.
For questions 16–20, solve the problem and enter your answer in the grid box.

NOTES

1. The use of a calculator **is not permitted**.
2. All variables and expressions used represent real numbers unless otherwise indicated.
3. Figures provided in this test are drawn to scale unless otherwise indicated.
4. All figures lie in a plane unless otherwise indicated.
5. Unless otherwise indicated, the domain of a given function f is the set of all real numbers x for which $f(x)$ is a real number.

REFERENCE

$A = \pi r^2$
$C = 2\pi r$

$A = \ell w$

$A = \frac{1}{2}bh$

$c^2 = a^2 + b^2$

Special Right Triangles

$V = \ell wh$

$V = \pi r^2 h$

$V = \frac{4}{3}\pi r^3$

$V = \frac{1}{3}\pi r^2 h$

$V = \frac{1}{3}\ell wh$

The number of degrees of arc in a circle is 360.
The number of radians of arc in a circle is 2π.
The sum of the measures in degrees of the angles of a triangle is 180.

CONTINUE ▶

2

$$6\left(y+\frac{1}{y}\right)-4\left(y+\frac{1}{y}\right)$$

Which of the following is equivalent to the expression above?

A) $\dfrac{2}{y}$

B) $2y+\dfrac{2}{y}$

C) $2y-\dfrac{2}{y}$

D) $2y$

4

An airplane takes off from a runway that is 55 meters above sea level. As the airplane rises to its cruising altitude, its height increases at an average rate of 6,000 feet per minute. Which of the following correctly models h, the height in feet of the plane above sea level, and m, the number of minutes after the plane takes off?

A) $h = 55m + 6,000$

B) $h = 6,000m + 55$

C) $h = 55m + \dfrac{110,000}{6,000}$

D) $h = 6,000m + \dfrac{110,000}{55}$

6

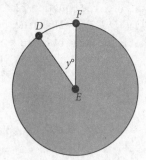

The circle in the figure above has center E, the area of unshaded minor sector DEF is 6π, and $y = 36$. What is the area of the shaded portion of the circle?

A) 27π

B) 30π

C) 54π

D) 60π

8

The equation $9(4p - 3) - 4(6p + 2) = 4cp + 30$ cannot be satisfied by any value of p. What is the value of the constant c?

A) 0

B) 3

C) 6

D) 9

CONTINUE

10

For all values of x, the equation $12x^3 - 59x^2 + 6x + 2 = (rx - 1)(3x^2 + 2sx - 2)$ is true. For constants r and s, what is the value of $r + s$?

A) -3

B) 7

C) 8

D) 16

12

Which of the following is equivalent to the expression $\dfrac{1}{3d-2} - 4$, for $d \neq \dfrac{2}{3}$?

A) $\dfrac{3d-6}{3d-2}$

B) $\dfrac{3d-4}{3d-2}$

C) $\dfrac{-12d+9}{3d-2}$

D) $\dfrac{-12d+8}{3d-2}$

CONTINUE

$$-15x + 5y \leq 20$$

$$y \leq \frac{1}{4}x + 8$$

The system of inequalities below can be graphed in the *xy*-plane. Which of the following correctly shows the solution set for the system of inequalities?

A)

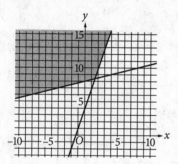

B)

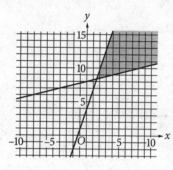

C)

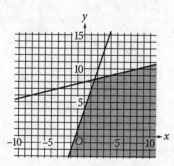

D)

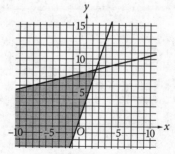

CONTINUE

DIRECTIONS

For questions 16–20, solve the problem and enter your answer in the grid, as described below, on the answer sheet.

1. Although not required, it is suggested that you write your answer in the boxes at the top of the columns to help you fill in the circles accurately. You will receive credit only if the circles are filled in correctly.

2. Mark no more than one circle in any column.

3. No question has a negative answer.

4. Some problems may have more than one correct answer. In such cases, grid only one answer.

5. **Mixed numbers** such as $3\frac{1}{2}$ must be gridded as 3.5 or 7/2. (If [3 1 / 2] is entered into the grid, it will be interpreted as $\frac{31}{2}$, not as $3\frac{1}{2}$.)

6. **Decimal Answers:** If you obtain a decimal answer with more digits than the grid can accommodate, it may be either rounded or truncated, but it must fill the entire grid.

Answer: $\frac{7}{12}$ Answer: 2.5

Write answer in boxes. ← Fraction line

Grid in result. ← Decimal point

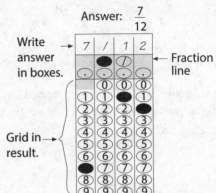
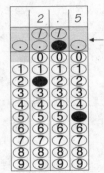

Acceptable ways to grid $\frac{2}{3}$ are:

Answer: 201 – either position is correct

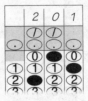
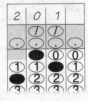

NOTE: You may start your answers in any column, space permitting. Columns you don't need to use should be left blank.

CONTINUE →

16

What is the width, in inches, of a rectangular solid that has a volume of 120 cubic inches, a length of 8 inches, and a height of 3 inches?

18

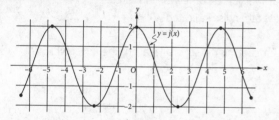

The function j is graphed in its entirety in the xy-plane in the figure above. The function k (not shown) is given as $k(x) = 17 - j(x)$. What is the value of function k when function j is at its minimum value?

20

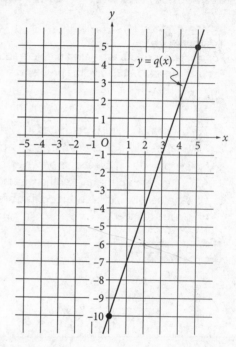

In the figure above, the linear function $q(x)$ is graphed in the xy-plane. The linear function n (not shown) passes through the point $(2, -6)$ and is perpendicular to the graph of q. What is the value of $n(-16)$?

STOP

If you finish before time is called, you may check your work on this section only.

Do not turn to any other section.

Math Test – Calculator

DIRECTIONS

For questions 1–30, solve each problem and choose the best answer from the choices provided.
For questions 31–38, solve the problem and enter your answer in the grid box.

NOTES

1. The use of a calculator **is permitted**.
2. All variables and expressions used represent real numbers unless otherwise indicated.
3. Figures provided in this test are drawn to scale unless otherwise indicated.
4. All figures lie in a plane unless otherwise indicated.
5. Unless otherwise indicated, the domain of a given function f is the set of all real numbers x for which $f(x)$ is a real number.

REFERENCE

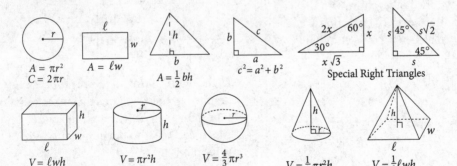

$A = \pi r^2$
$C = 2\pi r$

$A = \ell w$

$A = \frac{1}{2}bh$

$c^2 = a^2 + b^2$

Special Right Triangles

$V = \ell wh$

$V = \pi r^2 h$

$V = \frac{4}{3}\pi r^3$

$V = \frac{1}{3}\pi r^2 h$

$V = \frac{1}{3}\ell wh$

The number of degrees of arc in a circle is 360.
The number of radians of arc in a circle is 2π.
The sum of the measures in degrees of the angles of a triangle is 180.

CONTINUE

2

In ancient Greece, the obol and the drachma were used as currency, where 6 obols were equivalent to 1 drachma. If a house had an estimated value of 600 drachmas, approximately how many obols was the house estimated to be worth?

A) 3,600

B)   600

C)   100

D)   0.01

4

For the equation $\dfrac{1}{x} = -\sqrt{\left(\dfrac{1}{x}\right)^2}$, which of the following values of x is NOT a solution?

A) −4

B) −2

C) −1

D)   0

CONTINUE ➔

Questions 5 and 6 refer to the following information.

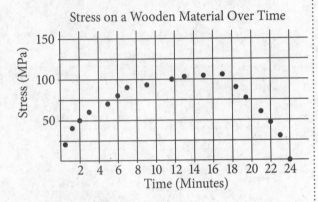

Stress on a Wooden Material Over Time

For a research project, a wooden material is subjected to varying amounts of stress over time to determine at what point the material will break. The breaking point is where the material breaks and stress begins to decrease until it reaches zero. The figure above shows the applied stress, in MPa, and the time in 2-minute intervals.

5

Which of the following best estimates the stress, in MPa, of the material when it reaches its breaking point?

A) 105

B) 90

C) 60

D) 0

6

During which of the following intervals of time, in minutes, does the stress increase at the least average rate?

A) Between 0 and 2 minutes

B) Between 3 and 6 minutes

C) Between 7 and 10 minutes

D) Between 14 and 16 minutes

CONTINUE

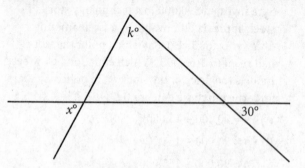

Note: Figure not drawn to scale

In the figure above, $x = 40$. What is the value of k?

A) 30

B) 40

C) 90

D) 110

An entomologist observed 105 insects and recorded whether or not each insect was black, and whether or not it was spotted. Based on the data shown in the table below, what is the probability that an insect selected at random from those observed by the entomologist did <u>not</u> have spots?

Insect Appearance Data

	Not spotted	Spotted	Total
Not Black	16	20	36
Black	14	23	37
Total	30	43	73

A) $\dfrac{30}{73}$

B) $\dfrac{16}{36}$

C) $\dfrac{14}{30}$

D) $\dfrac{16}{30}$

11

Rope 1 is 18 feet in length. Rope 2 is 27 feet in length. The ratio of the lengths of Rope 1 to Rope 2 is the same as the ratio of the lengths of Rope 3 to Rope 4. If Rope 4 is 54 feet long, how long, in feet, is Rope 3 ?

A) 31.5

B) 36.0

C) 45.0

D) 81.0

13

Steven sews suit jackets that have either 9 buttons or 12 buttons. To fill a window display, Steven needs to create at least 7 jackets. If Steven wants to make as many 12-button jackets as possible, and he has no more than 75 buttons, how many 12-button jackets can Steven make?

A) 3

B) 4

C) 5

D) 7

14

Sara invested $90,000 in a technology stock. The stock appreciated in value by a fixed amount every year for 5 years, at which point the value had risen to $165,000. Which equation below best models the price of the stock, p, in dollars, y years after the purchase date for $0 \leq y \leq 5$?

A) $p = 90{,}000 + 15{,}000y$

B) $p = 90{,}000 - 15{,}000y$

C) $p = 90{,}000 + 165{,}000y$

D) $p = 165{,}000 + 15{,}000y$

CONTINUE

Questions 18–20 refer to the following information.

Vivian is performing an experiment involving solutions mixed in specific proportions. She has created $\frac{2}{3}$-liter of solution S which contains 120 grams of salt. In this solution, 100 grams of the salt was supplied by sea water. One liter of solution S also contains exactly 55 milligrams of magnesium, which supplies 20% of the full amount required for Vivian's experiment.

For the experiment, Vivian combines a certain volume of solution S with a certain volume of solution T. Solution T contains 100 grams of salt per liter. The total amount of salt in one liter of the new solution is 160 grams. What volume of solution S is in one liter of the mixture?

A) $\frac{1}{4}$ liter

B) $\frac{1}{2}$ liter

C) $\frac{3}{4}$ liter

D) $\frac{7}{8}$ liter

If x percent of the magnesium required to complete the experiment is provided by y liters of solution S, how would x be expressed in terms of y ?

A) $x = (0.2)^y$

B) $x = (1.2)^y$

C) $x = 2y$

D) $x = 20y$

CONTINUE

Which of the following graphs could be a function relating the number of grams of salt from sea water in a given volume of solution S to the number of $\frac{2}{3}$-liter beakers of the solution?

A)

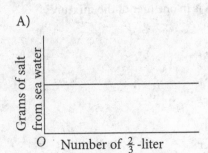

B)

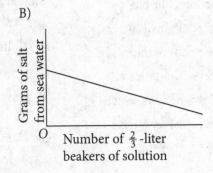

C)

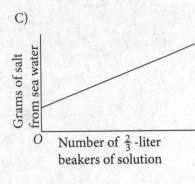

D)

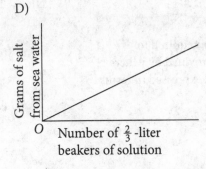

CONTINUE

In a U.S. magazine for dentistry professionals, the editor asked the magazine's readers to answer a poll, via email, asking the question, "Are the new government guidelines on fluoride usage sufficient?" In the issue that was published the following week, the magazine stated that 23% of respondents indicated "No" and 76% indicated "Yes." Which statement below best explains why it is unlikely the poll results represent the opinions of the entire population of the U.S.?

A) The percent of "Yes" responses did not equal the percent of "No" responses.

B) A week is not enough time for readers to email their responses.

C) The respondents to the poll did not make up a random sample of the population of the United States.

D) The percentages of respondents answering "No" and "Yes" make up less than 100%, so the conclusions drawn are not valid.

The height of a ball above the ground m, in meters, which was thrown t seconds ago, is modeled by the quadratic function $m(t) = -4.9t^2 + 25t + 8$. If $y = m(t)$ is graphed, what would the positive y-intercept, as depicted on the graph, represent?

A) The initial height of the ball

B) The maximum height the ball reaches

C) The number of seconds after which the projectile reaches maximum height

D) The number of seconds elapsed when the ball hits the ground

The graph below plots the length of an icicle each week starting on January 5th. A line of best fit is included which has the equation $y = -0.6x + 32$. Which statement about the decrease in the length of the icicle is supported by the line of best fit?

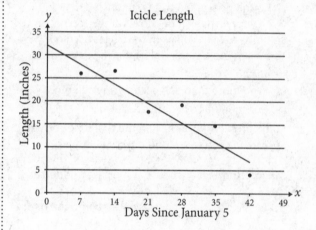

A) The length of the icicle decreased, on average, 32 inches every week.

B) The length of the icicle decreased, on average, 0.6 inches every week.

C) The length of the icicle decreased, on average, 32 inches every day.

D) The length of the icicle decreased, on average, 0.6 inches every day.

CONTINUE

DIRECTIONS

For questions 31–38, solve the problem and enter your answer in the grid, as described below, on the answer sheet.

1. Although not required, it is suggested that you write your answer in the boxes at the top of the columns to help you fill in the circles accurately. You will receive credit only if the circles are filled in correctly.

2. Mark no more than one circle in any column.

3. No question has a negative answer.

4. Some problems may have more than one correct answer. In such cases, grid only one answer.

5. **Mixed numbers** such as $3\frac{1}{2}$ must be gridded as 3.5 or 7/2. (If  is entered into the grid, it will be interpreted as $\frac{31}{2}$, not as $3\frac{1}{2}$.)

6. **Decimal Answers:** If you obtain a decimal answer with more digits than the grid can accommodate, it may be either rounded or truncated, but it must fill the entire grid.

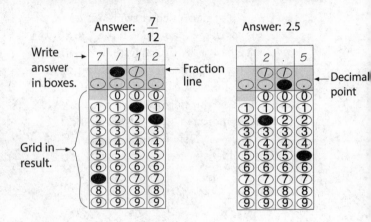

Answer: $\frac{7}{12}$ Answer: 2.5

Acceptable ways to grid $\frac{2}{3}$ are:

Answer: 201 – either position is correct

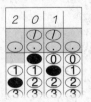

NOTE: You may start your answers in any column, space permitting. Columns you don't need to use should be left blank.

CONTINUE ▶

31

The center of the circle shown below in the *xy*-plane is at $(4, y)$.

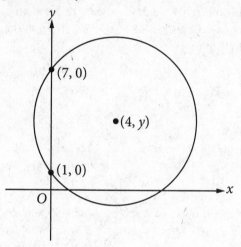

What is the radius of the circle?

33

A clothing company is selling T-shirts in five sizes: XS, S, M, L, and XL. The shirts come in two colors, red and blue. The chart below gives a summary of the number of shirt sizes and colors the company is shipping for the month of July.

Shirt color	Shirt Size				
	XS	S	M	L	XL
Red	25	35	50	55	30
Blue	20	30	40	x	30

If one blue shirt is selected at random, the probability that the size of the shirt is medium is $\frac{1}{4}$. What is the value of x in the table?

CONTINUE

Questions 37 and 38 refer to the following information.

Appliance	Save-a-Lot Price	Good Deals Price
Can opener	$12.00	$12.95
Hand mixer	$14.30	$15.50
Waffle iron	$18.50	$19.00
Toaster	$20.40	$21.45
Blender	$26.50	$27.60
Rice cooker	$29.95	$31.30
Pressure cooker	$52.00	$53.00

The table above gives the prices of seven different types of kitchen appliances as they appeared in advertisements from two different department stores.

37

According to the data, the median price at Save-a-Lot for the appliances listed in the table was how much less, in dollars, than the median price at Good Deals for the appliances listed in the table, to the nearest cent?

38

At Save-a-Lot, the price of a blender was 7% less than at Low Cost Appliances department store. The price of a blender was d dollars less at Save-a-Lot than at Low Cost Appliances. To the nearest dollar, what is the value of d ?

STOP

If you finish before time is called, you may check your work on this section only.

Do not turn to any other section.

Mini Practice Test:
Answers and Explanations

Mini Practice Test: Answers and Explanations

Reading Explanations

21. **D** The question asks why the author *uses the phrase "emotional contagion."* Use the given line reference to find the window. The text states that *rats are sensitive to each other's emotions, 'catching' them from one another*. Eliminate answers that don't match the prediction. Choice (A) refers to *mood disorders*, but the text never discusses *mood disorders*. Eliminate (A). Choice (B) refers to *the time in which rats learn to open the gates*, which is not mentioned in the window for this question. Eliminate (B). Choice (C) refers to the rats' *apathetic reaction*. "Apathy" means a lack of interest or emotional involvement, which is the opposite of what the passage states. Eliminate (C). Choice (D) refers to the *spread* of the emotions between the rats, which closely matches the prediction. The correct answer is (D).

22. **A** The question asks why *the rats were "stressed."* Use the given line reference to find the window. In the passage, the author states that the researcher placed one of the rats *in a cage* and that the *trapped rats were clearly stressed*. Eliminate answers that don't match the prediction. Choice (A) says that the rats were stressed because of the *restrained environment*, which closely matches the prediction. Keep (A). Choice (B) is a Right Answer, Wrong Question trap answer; the stressed, trapped rats were not the ones that faced *a learning task*—it was their partners that had to figure out how to free them. Eliminate (B). Choice (C) is also a Right Answer, Wrong Question trap answer, since it was the free rats who responded to *the emotional distress of their* trapped *cage-mates*. Eliminate (C). Choice (D) states that the rats were stressed because they *had been paired with an unfamiliar cage-mate*, but the passage states that the scientist *kept her rats in pairs for two weeks* before one of the rats was placed in a cage. Therefore, the rats were familiar with their cage-mates. Eliminate (D). The correct answer is (A).

23. **B** The question asks for the *best evidence* that *rats are motivated by factors other than empathy*. Use the line references given in the answer choices to find a statement that supports this claim. The lines for (A) discuss what the empathic rats did during the experiment, but it does not offer another motive for a rat's actions. Eliminate (A). The lines for (B) state that the rats *freed their cage-mate as often as they went for the food*. This means that not all of the rats were *motivated by empathy*. Some were more motivated by *food*. Keep (B). Choice (C) suggests that the rats were motivated by *empathy*, but the question asks for evidence that they were motivated by something *other than empathy*. Eliminate (C). Like the lines for (C), the lines for (D) suggest that the rats' motive was *empathy*. Eliminate (D). The correct answer is (B).

24. **D** The question asks about a *finding* that *would undermine Bartal's results*. Since there is no line reference, use the order of the questions to find the window. The answer to Q23 came from lines 31–33, and those lines describe Bartal's findings. The third paragraph states, *Bartal found that the rats spent more time exploring the cage, and were more likely to open it, when there was another rat inside. It didn't matter if the liberated rat got nothing in return. Even when the rats were faced with a second cage containing delicious chocolate chips, they freed their cage-mate as often as they went for the food.* From these results, it is concluded that *empathy is a powerful motivator.* Eliminate answers that do not weaken these findings. Choice (A) states that the amount of *maternal care* that mammals give their offspring corresponds with the amount of empathy they demonstrate in experimental settings. This finding would support a hypothesis given by *De Waal* in the last paragraph, but this question asks for a finding that *would undermine Bartal's results.* Eliminate (A). Eliminate (B) because it supports Bartal's finding that rats display empathy when they encounter another rat who is trapped. Choice (C) brings up *other species of rodents.* Although other mammals are discussed in the last paragraph, Bartal's findings were about *rats*, not about *other species of rodents*, so this finding would not undermine Bartal's results. Eliminate (C). Choice (D) shows that rats are more likely to open a cage with cheese than a cage with another rat in it. In Bartal's experiment, the rats were just as likely to open a cage with a trapped cage-mate as they were to open a cage with chocolate chips, but the finding in (D) shows that when offered a different food, the rats were more likely to go for the food than to help a trapped cage-mate. This undermines Bartal's findings, so keep (D). The correct answer is (D).

25. **A** The question asks what the word *underlie* most nearly means in line 67. Go back to the text, find the word *underlie*, and cross it out. Then read the window carefully, using context clues to determine another word that would fit in the text. The text says that *these [ancient neural] circuits underlie the behaviour of different mammals.* Therefore, *underlie* must mean something like "contribute to." *Influence* matches "contribute to," so keep (A). *Hide* does not match "contribute to," so eliminate (B). *Prove* does not match "contribute to," so eliminate (C). *Alter* means "change," which does not match "contribute to," so eliminate (D). The correct answer is (A).

26. **C** The question asks for a statement about *mammals* that is supported by Bartal's study. Notice that this is the first question in a paired set, so it can be done in tandem with Q27. Look at the answer choices for Q27 first. The lines for (27A) say that *Bartal has strengthened the case made by previous studies.* Although these lines suggest that Bartal's study supported some other findings, they don't mention any particular finding about *mammals.* Therefore, the information does not address Q26, so eliminate (27A). The lines for (27B) do not include a statement about mammals. The information does not address Q26, so eliminate (27B). The lines for (27C) refer

to the *circuits* that *underlie the behavior* of various animals. Check the answers for Q26 to see whether any of the answers are supported by these lines. This information does not support any of the answers for Q26, so eliminate (27C). The lines for (27D) discuss the difference between male and female rats' responses to a trapped rat, which supports (26C). Draw a line connecting (27D) and (26C). Without any support in the answers from Q27, (26A), (26B), and (26D) can be eliminated. The correct answers are (26C) and (27D).

27. **D** (See explanation above.)

28. **B** The question asks for the main purpose of the *last paragraph*. Read the last paragraph as the window. The paragraph discusses the *neural circuits* and *maternal care* that may explain the empathic behavior of rats and other mammals. Eliminate answers that don't match the prediction. Choice (A) refers to *previous studies, in which researchers found no evidence of empathy*. This contradicts what is written in the passage, so eliminate (A). Choice (B) refers to an *explanation for the results of the study*, which closely matches the prediction. Keep (B). Choice (C) is a Right Answer, Wrong Question trap answer; the paragraph does discuss brain pathways, but explaining their *role* in *mammals other than rats* is not the main purpose of the paragraph. Eliminate (C). Choice (D) states that the conclusion *challenges an existing scientific viewpoint*. No *viewpoint* is challenged in this paragraph, so eliminate (D). The correct answer is (B).

29. **B** The question asks *what percent of the session had occurred* before *males reacting to a trapped mate opened the door*, according to figure 1. First, look at the bar graph in figure 1 that is labelled *males trapped*. According to figure 1, less than 50% of the session had occurred. Eliminate (C) and (D) because they are over 50%. The bar is over halfway to 50%, so *between 10 and 20 percent* is too low; eliminate (A) and keep (B). The correct answer is (B).

30. **A** The question asks for a *conclusion about the mean activity of the rats* that is *supported by figure 2*. Work through each answer choice using the figure. Figure 2 includes four bars—two show the activity level for male and female rats reacting to an empty cage, and two show the activity level for male and female rats reacting to a cage with a trapped mate. Choice (A) states that *the contents of the cage had a greater effect on mean activity than did the rat's sex*. This is supported by the figure, as the difference between male and female rats in each pair of bars is fairly small, while the differences between the activity in response to an empty cage and the activity in response to a trapped rat are much larger. Keep (A). Choice (B) is contradicted by the figure: rats had higher activity levels, not *lower activity levels*, when responding to a trapped mate. Eliminate (B). Choice (C) is contradicted by the figure: the contents of the cage had a much greater impact on the rats' activity level than did their sex. While the males' activity level was slightly higher than the females' when responding to an empty cage, it did not *greatly exceed* the females' activity level. Furthermore, when responding to a trapped mate, the females' activity level was higher. Eliminate (D). The correct answer is (A).

31. **D** The question asks for a difference between *rats reacting to a cage containing a trapped mate* and *rats reacting to an empty cage*, according to figures 1 and 2. Work through each answer choice using the figures. Choice (A) refers to *distress over denial of food. Distress* is not recorded by either figure, so eliminate (A). Choice (B) states that rats reacting to an empty cage *open the cage sooner*, but this is contradicted by figure 1. Eliminate (B). Choice (C) refers to *empathic behavior*, which is not directly recorded by either figure. Furthermore, the passage indicates that opening a cage door for a trapped mate is empathic behavior, so a rat opening the door of an empty cage would not be displaying empathic behavior. Eliminate (C). Choice (D) states that rats reacting to an empty cage *open the cage later and have a lower activity level*, which is supported by both figures. The correct answer is (D).

32. **A** The question asks about the *main purpose* of the passage. Because this is a general question, it should be done after the specific questions. The first paragraph states that *the question of Woman's Rights is a practical one* and that women should be allowed to *find their sphere*. The second paragraph provides examples of women being paid less than men for their work. The third paragraph discusses benefits of a woman being able to *make money for herself*, and the final paragraph advocates for the *widening of women's sphere* and *a hand with a dollar and a quarter a day in it*. Therefore, the main purpose of the passage is to advocate for women's right to work and be paid fairly. Eliminate answers that don't match the prediction. Arguing for women's freedom *to choose their employment and be fairly compensated* matches the prediction. Keep (A). Choice (B) contradicts the passage, so eliminate it. The author does not mention *recreational activities*; eliminate (C). The text does not state that women should pursue *employment opportunities typically held by men*, just that they should be free to choose and be paid equally. Eliminate (D). The correct answer is (A).

33. **D** The question asks what *technique* Stone uses *to support her central point*. Because this is a general question, it should be done after the specific questions. In the second paragraph, Stone presents examples such as the fact that *women working in tailor shops are paid one-third as much as men* and that this leaves a woman *just three and a half cents a day for bread*. She also states that *female teachers in New York are paid fifty dollars a year, and for every such situation there are five hundred applications*. In the third paragraph, Stone argues that the *present condition of woman causes a horrible perversion of the marriage relation*. Therefore, Stone supports her central point with examples of problems caused by limited employment options and pay for women. Eliminate answers that don't match the prediction. The text does not indicate that Stone's beliefs *are already held by society*, so eliminate (A). Stone gives no *personal anecdotes*, so eliminate (B). In most of the examples, Stone discusses women who are not paid fairly, so eliminate (C). Choice (D) matches the prediction; Stone *presents a series of troubling conditions* regarding women's limited pay and employment options. The correct answer is (D).

34. **C** The question asks how the author develops her argument about *a limited woman's "sphere."* Since this is a general question, it should be answered after the specific questions. In the first paragraph, Stone states that doctrines about a *woman's sphere…have no basis except in the usages and prejudices of the age.* In the second paragraph, she describes how a woman is made *a dependent,* is discouraged from devoting herself *to some worthy purpose,* and is paid less than men. In the third paragraph, she describes how the *present condition of woman causes a horrible perversion of the marriage relation.* In other words, Stone argues that there is not a valid basis for the limitation of women's sphere, and then demonstrates the problems that the limitation causes. Eliminate answers that don't match the prediction. Stone does not explain the creation of the concept of *woman's sphere;* eliminate (A). While she does claim that *past definitions of the concept are* baseless, she does not say that they are *irrelevant,* and she does not state that women should *become more vocal.* Eliminate (B). Keep (C) because Stone does *refute* (which means "argue against") *the concept as baseless* and then continues to *illustrate* the problems that it causes. Eliminate (D) because, although Stone does imply that a limited sphere for women is widely accepted, she argues against it, not *in support of preserving it.* The correct answer is (C).

35. **D** The question asks about the basis for the *restrictions placed on women.* Notice that this is the first question in a paired set, so it can be done in tandem with Q36. Look at the answer choices for Q36 first. The lines for (36A) say that the author will *deepen this disappointment in every woman's heart until she bows down to it no longer.* Check the answers for Q35 to see whether any of the answers are supported by these lines. This statement doesn't support any of the answer choices in Q35, so eliminate (36A). The lines in (36B) say that the doctrines about a *woman's sphere…have no basis except in the usages and prejudices of the age.* These lines support (35D). Draw a line connecting (36B) and (35D). The lines for (36C) say that the author wants people to *leave women, then, to find their sphere.* This doesn't support any of the answer choices in Q35; eliminate (36C). The lines for (36D) say that a man is *held back by nothing but what is in himself,* which doesn't support any of the answer choices in Q35. Eliminate (36D). Without any support in the answers from Q36, (35A), (35B), and (35C) can be eliminated. The correct answers are (35D) and (36B).

36. **B** (See explanation above.)

37. **A** The question asks about *a distinction* Stone draws in the passage. Notice that this is the first question in a paired set, so it can be done in tandem with Q38. Look at the answer choices for Q38 first. The lines for (38A) say that *the notion has prevailed that* women's rights are *only an ephemeral idea.* (*Ephemeral* means "short-lived.") Check the answers for Q37 to see whether any of the answers are supported by these lines. This statement doesn't support any of the answer choices in Q37, so eliminate (38A). The lines for (38B) say that women *mistake the politeness of men for rights.* These lines support (37A). Draw a line connecting (37A) and (38B).

The lines for (38C) say that *the same society that drives forth the young man, keeps woman at home.* This statement does not support any of the answer choices in Q38. At first glance, it might seem to support (37D), but the statement is not about the activities that are *preferred* by women and men. Eliminate (38C). The lines for (38D) state that *female teachers in New York are paid fifty dollars a year, and for every such situation there are five hundred applications.* Although these lines mention *employment opportunities in New York*, they do not mention a difference between New York and *Philadelphia*. These lines don't support any of the answer choices in Q37, so eliminate (38D). Without any support in the answers from Q38, (37B), (37C), and (37D) can be eliminated. The correct answers are (37A) and (38B).

38. **B** (See explanation above.)

39. **A** The question asks what *the main effect of the use of the word "sufferers"* is in line 63. Use the given line reference to find the window. The passage states that *men are the sufferers* because *a woman who loathes you may marry you because you have the means to get money which she can not have.* In other words, men are harmed because women need to marry for financial security rather than for love. Eliminate answers that don't match the prediction. Keep (A) because it mentions *harm done to men.* The passage does not state that *men's roles* are *restrictive*; eliminate (B). The *sufferers* mentioned in these lines are men, not *women*, so eliminate (C). The author does not mention a *global perspective* in the window for the question. Eliminate (D). The correct answer is (A).

40. **B** The question asks what *goal* must be met before a *woman may marry a man out of a sense of affection*. Since there is no line reference, use lead words and the order of the questions to find the window. Q39 asks about line 63. Scan the third paragraph, looking for the lead words *marry* and *affection*. In lines 66–68, the passage states *when a woman can enter the lists with you and make money for herself, she will marry you only for deep and earnest affection.* In other words, women will be able to marry out of a sense of affection when they can earn their own money. Eliminate answers that don't match the prediction. The passage does not state that a woman needs to *contribute more* financially than her husband does, so eliminate (A). Choice (B) matches the prediction that women need to earn their own money before marrying for love; keep it. Choice (C) is a Right Words, Wrong Meaning trap answer: the passage does not state that women will ease men's suffering by *taking on more financial responsibility*. Instead, it indicates that men's suffering is caused by the fact that women who don't love them may marry them. Eliminate (C). Eliminate (D) because the text discusses women's employment and earning, rather than women's satisfaction with their husbands' jobs and salaries. The correct answer is (B).

41. **C** The question asks for the best summary of the final paragraph. Carefully read the final paragraph. In it, Stone describes *a woman at manual labor turning out chair-legs in a cabinetshop*. She goes on to express her wish that *other women would imitate her in this,* saying, *I think a hand with a dollar and a quarter a day in it, better than one with a crossed ninepence.... The widening of woman's sphere is to improve her lot*. Eliminate answers that don't match the prediction. In this paragraph, Stone does not discuss an issue that *has been problematic throughout history*, so eliminate (A). Although Stone does mention what she wishes women would do, she does not *provide a detailed plan to fix* the issue at hand, so eliminate (B). Choice (C) matches the text: the description of the woman working in the cabinetshop is a *particular example*, and Stone does broaden the example by expressing her wish that *other women* would do the same, and arguing that the good pay associated with the manual labor is better than lower pay. She uses the example to support her central claim that women will improve their situations by *widening* their *sphere*. Keep (C). Eliminate (D) because the final paragraph does not include a *commonly held view*, and Stone argues against the commonly held view of women's sphere throughout the speech. The correct answer is (C).

42. **B** The question asks what the word *detaining* most nearly means in line 70. Go back to the text, find the word *detaining,* and cross it out. Then read the window carefully, using context clues to determine another word that would fit in the text. The text says, *I am detaining you too long, many of you standing, that I ought to apologize.* Therefore, *detaining* must mean something like "causing to stay." *Obstructing* means "blocking one's path"; this does not match the prediction, so eliminate (A). *Keeping* matches "causing to stay," so keep (B). *Arresting* means "taking under control by authority of law"; this does not match the prediction, so eliminate (C). *Hindering* means "preventing" someone from doing something; this doesn't match the prediction, so eliminate (D). Note that (A), (C), and (D) are Could Be True trap answers based on other meanings of *detaining* that are not supported by the text. The correct answer is (B).

43. **A** The question asks what *advantage of using the LENS® technique to manufacture implants* is suggested by the author. Notice that this is the first question in a paired set, so it can be done in tandem with Q44. Look at the answer choices for Q44 first. The lines for (44A) describe the LENS® process, including the fact that *custom parts can be quickly built up layer by layer*. Check the answers for Q43 to see whether any of the answers are supported by these lines. These lines do not support any of the answers in Q43, so eliminate (44A). The lines for (44B) say, *The process is so precise that parts can be used straight off the printer without the polishing or finishing needed in traditional manufacturing*. This information matches (43A): since no *polishing or finishing* is required, the process is *more efficient*. Draw a line connecting (44B) and (43A). The lines for (44C) are about *bone*. These lines do not address Q43, so eliminate (44C). The lines for (44D) say, *LENS® can be used to make parts out of many different materials, including metals and ceramics*. Although (43D) does mention *material*, it says that the LENS® technique uses *a single material*. Eliminate (44D). Without any support in the answers from Q44, (43B), (43C), and (43D) can be eliminated. The correct answers are (43A) and (44B).

44. **B** (See explanation above.)

45. **D** The question asks for the purpose of the fourth paragraph. Use the given line reference to find the window. The fourth paragraph discusses *a significant problem with today's implants*, specifically how *a metal implant is much stiffer* than the surrounding bones, so the *bones weaken and break down*. Eliminate answers that don't match the prediction. Eliminate (A) because the fourth paragraph does not discuss a *hypothesis*, and it does not counter *real-world data* from the earlier paragraphs. Eliminate (B) because the fourth paragraph is not a *conclusion*; it introduces a new topic. Eliminate (C) because the fourth paragraph does not discuss *an exceptional case*. Keep (D) because the fourth paragraph does discuss *a problem*, and the next paragraph discusses how *LENS®* technology may solve the problem by using *many different materials*. The correct answer is (D).

46. **D** The question asks what the word *implications* most nearly means in line 74. Go back to the text, find the word *implications*, and cross it out. Then read the window carefully, using context clues to determine another word that would fit in the text. The text says that 3D printing *has transformative implications for the future of health care*. Therefore, *implications* must mean something like "effects." *Connotations* means "associated qualities" and does not match "effects," so eliminate (A). *Inferences* means "conclusions" and does not match "effects," so eliminate (B). *Methods* means "procedures" and does not match "effects," so eliminate (C). *Consequences* matches "effects," so keep (D). Note that (A) and (B) are Could Be True trap answers based on other meanings of *implications* that are not supported by the text. The correct answer is (D).

47. **A** The question asks which *statement about 3D printing technology* the author of Passage 2 would most likely agree with. Use the order of the questions to find the window. Q46 asks about line 74, so the window for Q47 most likely begins after line 74. Eliminate answers that don't match the statements in the passage. Keep (A) because lines 83–88 state, *Advances in computer design and the ability to translate medical imaging—such as X-rays, computerized tomography (CT), magnetic resonance imaging (MRI) or ultrasound—to digital models that can be read by 3D printers are expanding its applications in health care*. This information supports the claim that 3D printing will be used in conjunction with (which means "together with") *other types of medical technology*. Choice (B) is a Mostly Right, Slightly Wrong answer: the passage says that 3D printing may *decrease* costs, not increase costs, *by disrupting supply chains*. Eliminate (B). Eliminate (C) because the passage doesn't focus on *traditional manufacturing*. Eliminate (D) because it is contradicted by the passage: the author states that advances in 3D printing technology *are already changing health care*. The correct answer is (A).

48. **B** The question asks why the author of Passage 2 *uses the phrase "far away from surgery on Mars."* Use the given reference from the passage to find the window. The last sentence of the passage says, *Although we may be far away from surgery on Mars using 3D printing technology, the advances on earth are already changing health care.* Eliminate answers that don't match the prediction. Eliminate (A) because there is no mention of *governments* or *space exploration* in the window. Choice (B) says that the purpose of the phrase is to *highlight the benefits* of 3D printing technology. This matches the prediction that advances *are already changing healthcare.* Choice (B) also mentions an *earlier reference,* so scan the rest of the passage for the lead word *Mars.* The first paragraph of Passage 2 is a hypothetical application of 3D printing for an astronaut on Mars. Keep (B). Eliminate (C) because according to the passage, *3D printing on Mars* is not possible yet; therefore, the passage does not *contrast the uses of 3D printing technology on Mars with its uses on other planets.* Eliminate (D) because the passage says *surgery on Mars* is *far away,* not *unrealistic.* The correct answer is (B).

49. **B** The question asks for the best description of *the relationship between Passage 1 and Passage 2.* Because this is a question about both passages, it should be done after the questions that ask about each passage individually. Passage 1 is about the LENS® process of manufacturing medical implants. Passage 2 is about 3D printing and the future of healthcare. Eliminate (A) because the *process* is described in Passage 1, not Passage 2. Keep (B) because the LENS® process is a *specific example* of 3D printing. Eliminate (C) because Passage 1 does not *cast doubt on the cost effectiveness* of 3D printing. Eliminate (D) because Passage 1 does not discuss *experimental results* and Passage 2 does not discuss a *theory.* The correct answer is (B).

50. **C** The question asks what point both passages make about how *3D printing could be useful.* Because this is a question about both passages, it should be done after the questions that ask about each passage individually. Eliminate (A) because neither passage says that 3D printing can help *determine exactly how the human body will respond to any implant.* Eliminate (B) because, although Passage 1 does discuss the *natural breakdown of bones,* it does not mention *organs.* Passage 2 mentions *organs,* but not their breakdown. Keep (C) because lines 6–13 of Passage 1 say that the 3-D printers are being used to create implants that *can be custom-designed for unusual injuries or anatomy,* and lines 91–94 of Passage 2 say that 3D printing *allows for personalization of health care,* including *customized prostheses.* Eliminate (D) because Passage 1 does not discuss *surgeries.* The correct answer is (C).

51. **D** The question asks what *conclusion about the hypothetical LENS® implant discussed in Passage 1* is supported by *information in Passage 2.* Because this is a question about both passages, it should be done after the questions that ask about each passage individually. Notice that this is the first question in a paired set, so it can be done in tandem with Q52. Look at the answer choices for Q52 first. The lines for (52A) discuss the hypothetical example of an astronaut

breaking a bone on Mars. This information does not support any of the answer choices in Q51, so eliminate (52A). The lines for (52B) state, *This layering capability allows the manufacturing of complex shapes, such as the intricate structure of bones or vascular channels, that would be impossible to create by other methods.* This information matches (51D), supporting the idea that the *implant's structure* could not be created using *traditional methods*. Draw a line connecting (52B) and (51D). The lines for (52C) discuss translating *medical images* to *digital models* for 3D printing. Although those lines may seem to support (51A), since they mention specific types of *medical images*, the lines do not say that it is *most effective* to combine them. Therefore, the lines for (52C) do not support any of the answers for Q51. Eliminate (52C). The lines for (52D) indicate that 3D printing can *decrease costs*, but none of the answer choices in Q51 mention costs; therefore, (52D) does not support any of the answers for Q51. Eliminate (52D). Without any support in the answers from Q52, (51A), (51B), and (51C) can be eliminated. The correct answers are (51D) and (52B).

52.　**B**　(See explanation above.)

Writing and Language Explanations

1. **C** Wording is changing in the answer choices, so the question is testing consistency. The sentence contains the comparison word *as*, and a comparison must compare the same kinds of things. The two things being compared are *its hostile interior* and *the Sahara Desert*. Choices (A) and (B) use the words *those of* and *that of*, but there are no nouns that *those* or *that* could refer back to, so eliminate (A) and (B). Choice (D) is redundant because the sentence already includes the word *dry*. Choice (C) is concise and makes a correct comparison. The correct answer is (C).

2. **B** Transitions are changing in the answer choices, so this question is testing consistency of ideas. A transition must be consistent with the relationship between the ideas it connects. The sentence before the transition states that most of the *species* in Antarctica *are concentrated in the waters and areas near the coast*, and the sentence that starts with the transition states that *the few creatures that do survive on the mainland of Antarctica thrive in large numbers*. These sentences draw a contrast between *most* creatures and the *few* on the mainland, so eliminate any answer choices that include same-direction transitions. *Similarly* implies that the second idea is similar to the first, but the two sentences discuss different types of *creatures*. Eliminate (A). Keep (B) because it appropriately uses the contrasting transition *However*. *Thus* implies that the second sentence is a conclusion drawn from information in the first sentence, which is not true. Eliminate (C). *Moreover* implies that the second sentence will add additional information that agrees with the information in the first sentence. Since the second sentence does not provide new details that add to the first sentence, eliminate (D). The correct answer is (B).

3. **D** Pronouns are changing in the answer choices, so this question is testing consistency of pronouns. A pronoun must be consistent in number with the noun it refers to. The underlined pronoun refers to the word *Their* (the *few creatures on the mainland of Antarctica* mentioned in the previous sentence), which is plural. To be consistent, the underlined pronoun must also be plural. Eliminate (A) and (C) because *it* and *one* are both singular pronouns. The pronouns *he or she* can only be used to refer to a person (not a creature), and both are singular pronouns, so eliminate (B). Keep (D) because *them* is a plural pronoun that can refer to the creatures. The correct answer is (D).

4. **D** Apostrophes are changing in the answer choices, so the question is testing apostrophe usage. When used with a noun, on the SAT, an apostrophe indicates possession. In this sentence, only one *continent* (Antarctica) is being discussed, so it is singular. The *microbes* belong to the *continent*, so an apostrophe is needed with *continent*. Because *continent* is singular, the apostrophe should be placed before the *s*. Eliminate (A) because it does not contain the apostrophe. Eliminate (B) because the apostrophe is after the *s*, which implies that more than one continent contains the *microbes*. Since both (C) and (D) appropriately place the apostrophe before the *s* to form *continent's*, consider the second word. Nothing belongs to the *microbes*, so there is no need to use an apostrophe. Eliminate (C). The correct answer is (D).

5. **B** Note the question! The question asks whether a sentence should be revised, so it's testing consistency. If the content of the new phrase is more consistent with the ideas surrounding it than the existing phrase is, the sentence should be revised. The paragraph discusses how *microbes* have adapted to survive in an environment with *very few nutrients*, and the sentence provides evidence to support this idea. The current sentence states that the microbes have *evolved to survive*, but the new phrase provides a reason why this evolution is so special: the microbes *survive only on air*. Since the new phrase is consistent with the ideas in the text and adds a relevant detail, the revision should be made. Eliminate (C) and (D). Eliminate (A) because the sentence does not explain *the origin of the microbes in Antarctica*. Keep (B) because it accurately states that the new phrase helps support the paragraph's main point. The correct answer is (B).

6. **C** The length of the phrase is changing in the answer choices, so this question is testing precision and concision. First determine what meaning of the phrase is necessary. The non-underlined portion of the sentence says that *organisms are able to harvest trace amounts* of certain gases *from the air*, and the underlined portion is part of a list of the gases harvested (carbon monoxide, hydrogen, and carbon dioxide). Since all three gases are part of the same list, all three are harvested. There is no need to interrupt the list by repeating the word *harvest* before *carbon dioxide*. Eliminate (A), (B), and (D) because each repeats the word *harvest* (or *harvesting*). Choice (C) is concise and makes the meaning of the sentence precise. The correct answer is (C).

7. **D** Punctuation is changing in the answer choices, so this question is testing punctuation rules. The sentence's main point is that the *nematode…uses an adaptation that allows it to survive its environment's extremely cold temperatures*. The phrase *along with other terrestrial invertebrates in Antarctica* is extra information that is not necessary to the meaning of the sentence. Therefore, the phrase should be surrounded by matching punctuation marks that separate it from the rest of the sentence. Since there is a long dash before the phrase, there should be a long dash after it to match. Eliminate (A), (B), and (C) because none of these has a long dash. The correct answer is (D).

8. **B** Note the question! The question asks how to effectively combine the underlined sentences, so it's testing precision and concision. The end of the first sentence says that *the worm produces a protein in its cells that cushions the ice*, and the second sentence says that the *protein prevents* the cells *from rupturing*. Therefore, the combined sentence should indicate that the protein does two things: it *cushions the ice* and *prevents the cells from rupturing*. Start with the shortest answer, which is (B). Choice (B) uses the word *and* to preserve the idea that the protein does two things, so it is correct and concise. Keep (B). The remaining answer choices add additional words but do not make the meaning of the sentence more precise. Eliminate (A), (C), and (D). The correct answer is (B).

9. **A** The length of the phrase is changing in the answer choices, so this question is testing precision and concision. First determine what meaning of the underlined portion is necessary. The non-underlined portion of the sentence suggests that *nematodes* are able to get rid of *the water from their bodies*, so there is no need to repeat that idea. Keep (A) because it is concise and makes the meaning of the sentence precise. Eliminate (B) because *eliminate* and *remove* mean the same thing in this context. Likewise, eliminate (D) because *eliminate* and *get rid of* also mean the same thing in this context. Eliminate (C) because the fact that the nematodes are *able to* rid their bodies of water means that they can remove water *capably*, so there is no need to repeat this idea. The correct answer is (A).

10. **C** Note the question! The question asks which choice *most effectively sets up the information in the next sentence*, so it's testing consistency of ideas. Determine the subject of the next sentence and find the answer that is consistent with that idea. The next sentence draws a comparison between *Antarctica* and *planets such as Mars*, based on the fact that both *feature extreme temperatures and lack water and nutrients*. Eliminate (A) because the long-standing beliefs of *researchers* don't set up the comparison between *Antarctica* and *planets such as Mars*. Eliminate (B) because it focuses on the *environmental niches* of *organisms all over the world* instead of on the comparison of environments between Antarctica and Mars-like planets. Keep (C) because it explains that the finding from Antarctica could be useful to *scientists* because it may help them *to evaluate the possibility of life on other planets*. Eliminate (D) because it does not relate Antarctica to environments on other planets. The correct answer is (C).

11. **C** Note the question! The question asks where sentence 4 should be placed, so it's testing consistency of ideas. The sentence must be consistent with the ideas that come both before and after it. Sentence 4 mentions *This total darkness*, so it must come after some mention of a *darkness*. Sentence 1 says that *Antarctica experiences months without sunlight* in the *winter*, which implies that it is totally dark in the winter. Therefore, sentence 4 should follow sentence 1. The correct answer is (C).

12. **A** Vocabulary is changing in the answer choices, so this question is testing precision of word choice. Look for a phrase with a definition that is consistent with the other ideas in the sentence. The sentence says that school districts are *worried about retaining teachers but unable or unwilling to increase salaries*, and that they are *looking for ways to provide* something *that might keep teachers in their districts*. The tone of the passage is formal, so eliminate choices that are informal. Eliminate (B) and (D) because *sweet* and *cool* are both too casual for the tone of the passage. Choices (A) and (C) both mean essentially the same thing: schools want to provide more things that will make teachers want to stay. Since both choices have a similar meaning, choose the one that is more concise. Eliminate (C). The correct answer is (A).

13. **C** Note the question! The question asks which choice *is the most effective version of the underlined portion*, so it's testing consistency. Notice that the words in each choice are fairly similar, but the order changes. In order to be effective, the correct answer must have the word order that makes the meaning clear and is concise. Eliminate (B) and (D) because they both use the word *teachers* twice, which is overly repetitive. Eliminate (A) because it is wordy compared to (C): it uses passive voice and contains extra words that don't help to clarify the meaning. Keep (C) because placing the subject (*teachers*) at the beginning of the phrase makes the meaning of this sentence most clear, and this answer is concise. The correct answer is (C).

14. **A** Pronouns and nouns are changing in the answer choices, so this question is testing precision. A pronoun can only be used if it is clear what the pronoun refers to. The pronouns *some*, *those*, or *they* could each refer to *A reduction in housing costs* or to *a pay increase*, so none of these pronouns is precise; eliminate (B), (C), and (D). In addition, each of these is plural, but the noun they should refer back to (*A reduction*) is singular. *Such an incentive* is singular and clearly refers to the previously mentioned teacher housing programs. Therefore, (A) is the most precise choice. The correct answer is (A).

15. **B** Punctuation and words are changing in the answer choices, so the question is testing punctuation rules and precision. Consider the two parts of the sentence in (A). The first part of the sentence, *According to the Economic Policy Institute, teacher salaries, adjusted for inflation, have fallen since the 1990s*, is a complete idea. The second part of the sentence, *those of other college graduates rose by over 100 dollars per week*, is a complete idea. Eliminate (A) because of the word *but* proceeded by a semicolon. The two ideas could be linked with a semicolon (which works just like a period) or with a comma and the word *but*, but a semicolon and *but* cannot be used. Keep (B) because a comma followed by *but* acts the same way a period does: it separates two complete ideas. Eliminate (C) because a comma alone cannot come between two complete ideas: this creates a run-on sentence. Choice (D) adds the word *however*, but the phrase *however, those of other college graduates rose by over 100 dollars per week* is still complete, so the comma still cannot be used. Eliminate (D). The correct answer is (B).

16. **D** Note the question! The question asks which choice *provides the best introduction to the paragraph*, so it's testing consistency of ideas. Determine the subject of the paragraph and find the answer that is consistent with that idea. The paragraph discusses several problems with teacher housing (for example, *housing built for teachers doesn't always go to teachers* and *the number of apartments or houses available is far lower than the number of teachers in the district*). Eliminate (A) because how well housing meets *teachers' needs* isn't discussed in this paragraph. Eliminate (B) because the paragraph focuses on teachers, not *other people seeking low-income housing*. Eliminate (C) because *oversight* and *community leaders* are never

mentioned in the paragraph. Keep (D) because it says that teacher housing *may also house too few teachers to make a significant impact*, which is a problem discussed in this paragraph. The correct answer is (D).

17. **B** Punctuation and words are changing in the answer choices, so the question is testing punctuation rules and precision. Consider the two parts of the sentence in (A). The first part of the sentence, *Although teacher housing has been implemented in various counties across the country*, is not a complete idea. The second part of the sentence, *housing built for teachers doesn't always go to teachers*, is a complete idea. Eliminate (A) because a semicolon functions like a period, but the first part of the sentence is not a complete sentence, so it couldn't have a period or semicolon after it. Keep (B) because a comma can follow an idea that is not complete. Eliminate (C) and (D) because a comma followed by *and* can only follow a complete idea. The correct answer is (B).

18. **C** Punctuation and words are changing in the answer choices, so the question is testing punctuation rules and precision. Consider the two parts of the sentence in (A). The first part of the sentence, *In Los Angeles, teacher housing was built using federal subsidies (a common practice for building teacher housing), but teachers weren't able to rent any of the apartments*, is a complete idea. The second part of the sentence, *Since the teachers' salaries were too high to qualify for low-income housing*, is not a complete idea. Eliminate (A) because the phrase *Since the teachers' salaries were too high to qualify for low-income housing* is not a complete sentence, so it needs to be part of the same sentence as the earlier phrase. Likewise, eliminate (D) because a semicolon functions in the same way a period does. Choices (B) and (C) eliminate the word *since*, so consider the parts of the sentence without this word. The first part of the sentence is still a complete idea, and the second part (*the teachers' salaries were too high to qualify for low-income housing*) is now also a complete idea. Eliminate (B) because a comma alone can't come between two complete ideas—this creates a run-on sentence. Keep (C) because a colon can separate two complete ideas. The correct answer is (C).

19. **B** Note the question! The question asks which choice *provides an accurate interpretation of the chart*, so it's testing consistency. Read the labels on the table carefully, and look for an answer that is consistent with the information given in the table. The sentence discusses *Newark, NJ*, so look at that row in the chart. Choice (A) says that *the district can provide housing for 2,700 teachers,* but the chart says that the district has 2,700 teachers and can only provide housing for 204 of them. Eliminate (A). Keep (B) because the chart indicates that 2,496 teachers will be without access to the housing. Eliminate (C) because the chart says that the district *can house* 7.5 percent of teachers, not *all but 7.5 percent* of them. Eliminate (D) because the chart says that the school district has 2,700 teachers, not 2,496. The correct answer is (B).

20. **D** Note the question! The question asks whether a sentence should be added, so it's testing consistency. If the content of the new sentence is consistent with the ideas surrounding it, then it should be added. Earlier in the paragraph, the author states that *the number of apartments or houses available is far lower than the number of teachers in the district.* The new sentence uses the phrase *on the other hand* to draw a contrast, and it states that *only* 570 teachers wouldn't be housed in Santa Clara, which implies that the lack of housing isn't a problem. Although it is true that this district leaves a smaller number of teachers without housing, this statement doesn't support the author's argument that many teachers are left out from housing and that this is a problem. Therefore, the author should not add this sentence. Eliminate (A) and (B). Eliminate (C) because there is no earlier *claim about housing subsidies* earlier in the paragraph that relates to this sentence. Keep (D) because it correctly states that the new sentence does not support the author's claim that many teachers are left out, since it uses the word *only* to minimize the number. The correct answer is (D).

21. **C** Verbs are changing in the answer choices, so this question is testing consistency of verbs. A verb must be consistent in tense with the other verbs in the sentence. The other verbs in the sentence (*find* and *can*) are in present tense, so the underlined verb should also be in present tense to be consistent. Eliminate (A) because *will not need* is in future tense. Eliminate (B) because *did not need* is in past tense. Keep (C) because *do not need* is in present tense. Eliminate (D) because *could not have needed* is in past tense. The correct answer is (C).

22. **A** Note the question! The question asks which choice *provides the best conclusion to the passage*, so it's testing consistency of ideas. Determine the subject of the passage and find the answer that is consistent with that idea. The passage discusses the pros and cons of teacher housing and suggests that the current models of teacher housing are not effective for teacher retention in most cases. Keep (A) because it says that teacher housing is *not a universal solution* to the problem of teacher retention, which is consistent with the passage. Eliminate (B) because the passage never mentions *new teachers* specifically. Eliminate (C) because the passage does not compare *houses* and *apartments*. Eliminate (D) because the passage mentions one study from the *Economic Policy Institute*, but this is not the main focus of the passage, so (D) is not consistent with the purpose stated in this question. The correct answer is (A).

Math No Calculator Explanations

2. **B** The question asks for an equivalent form of expression. Since the expression in both sets of the parentheses is the same, focus on the coefficients in front of the parentheses. To simplify the expression, subtract $6\left(y + \dfrac{1}{y}\right) - 4\left(y + \dfrac{1}{y}\right)$ to get $2\left(y + \dfrac{1}{y}\right)$. Distribute the 2 to the terms in the parentheses to get $2y + \dfrac{2}{y}$. Another way is to use Plugging In since there are variables in the answer choices. Either way, the correct answer is (B).

4. **B** The question asks for an equation that models a specific situation. Translate the information in Bite-Size Pieces and eliminate after each piece. One piece of information says the runway *is 55 meters above sea level*. This represents the initial height of the airplane, or the *y*-intercept. The *y*-intercept is the constant at the end of the equation when the equation is in $y = mx + b$ form. This only appears in (B), so eliminate (A), (C), and (D). The correct answer is (B).

6. **C** The question asks for the area of a part of the circle. Use the information about the smaller sector to find the area of the entire circle, then subtract the area of the smaller sector. The parts of a circle have a proportional relationship. In a circle, the fraction of the degrees in the smaller region is the same as the fraction of the sector area of the total area. Set up the proportion $\dfrac{\text{degrees}}{360°} = \dfrac{\text{sector area}}{\text{total area}}$, then plug in the given information to get $\dfrac{36°}{360°} = \dfrac{6\pi}{\text{total area}}$. Since calculator use is not allowed, reduce the fraction on the left to $\dfrac{1}{10}$. The proportion becomes $\dfrac{1}{10} = \dfrac{6\pi}{\text{total area}}$. Cross-multiply to get $10(6\pi) = 1(\textit{total area})$, or $60\pi = \textit{total area}$. Subtract the area of the smaller sector *DEF* from the total area of the circle. The area of the shaded part is $60\pi - 6\pi = 54\pi$. The correct answer is (C).

8. **B** The question asks for the value of a constant in an equation. Since the question asks for a specific value and the answers contain numbers in increasing order, plug in the answers. Begin by labeling the answer choices "*c*" and start with (B), **3**. The equation becomes $9(4p - 3) - 4(6p + 2) = 4(3)p + 30$. Distribute the coefficients to get $36p - 27 - 24p - 8 = 12p + 30$, and combine like terms to get $12p - 35 = 12p + 30$. The question states that the equation *cannot*

be satisfied by any value of p. This means there is no value of p that would solve the equation since the coefficients with the variable p are the same, and the constants are different. Since 12p on the left side is equal to 12p on the right side, stop here. The correct answer is (B).

10. **A** The question asks for the value of an expression. When given an equation in factored form, it is often necessary to multiply the factors out to standard form to solve the question. Since the right side of the equation is in factored form, distribute each term in the first set of parentheses to the second set of parentheses, then combine like terms. The equation becomes

$$12x^3 - 59x^2 + 6x + 2 = rx(3x^2 + 2sx - 2) - 1(3x^2 + 2sx - 2)$$

$$12x^3 - 59x^2 + 6x + 2 = 3rx^3 + 2rsx^2 - 2rx - 3x^2 - 2sx + 2$$

Gather like terms to make it easier to combine like terms, where the equation becomes

$$12x^3 - 59x^2 + 6x + 2 = 3rx^3 + 2rsx^2 - 3x^2 - 2rx - 2sx + 2$$

Combine like terms to get

$$12x^3 - 59x^2 + 6x + 2 = 3rx^3 + (2rs - 3)x^2 - 2(r + s)x + 2$$

The question asks for the value of $r + s$. The term that contains $r + s$ on the right side of the equation is $-2(r + s)x$. This corresponds to the $6x$ term on the left side of the equation. Set those terms equal to get $-2(r + s)x = 6x$. Solve for the expression $r + s$ by dividing both sides of the equation by x to get $-2(r + s) = 6$. Divide both sides by -2 to get $r + s = -3$. The correct answer is (A).

12. **C** The question asks for an equivalent form of an expression. There are variables in the answer choices, so plug in. Make $d = 2$. The expression becomes $\frac{1}{3(2) - 2} - 4 = \frac{1}{6 - 2} - 4 = \frac{1}{4} - 4 = \frac{1}{4} - \frac{16}{4} = -\frac{15}{4}$. This is the target value; circle it. Now plug $d = 2$ into the answer choices to see which one matches the target value. Choice (A) becomes $\frac{3(2) - 6}{3(2) - 2} = \frac{6 - 6}{6 - 2} = \frac{0}{4} = 0$. This does not match the target value, so eliminate

(A). Choice (B) becomes $\dfrac{3(2)-4}{3(2)-2} = \dfrac{6-4}{6-2} = \dfrac{2}{4} = \dfrac{1}{2}$. Eliminate (B). Choice (C) becomes

$\dfrac{-12(2)+9}{3(2)-2} = \dfrac{-24+9}{6-2} = \dfrac{-15}{4}$. This matches the target value, so keep (C) but check the

remaining answer just in case. Choice (D) becomes $\dfrac{-12(2)+8}{3(2)-2} = \dfrac{-24+8}{6-2} = \dfrac{-16}{4} = -4$.

Eliminate (D). The correct answer is (C).

14. **C** The question is asking for the solution set of a system of inequalities graphed in the coordinate plane. To determine which graph matches the given set of inequalities, solve the first inequality for y. Add $15x$ to both sides to get $5y \le 15x + 20$. Divide both sides of the inequality by 5 to get $y \le 3x + 4$. When graphing inequalities, the solution is represented by shading the area that is either above or below the inequality. In general, if y is less than the equation of the inequality, shade below the line. If y is greater than the equation of the inequality, shade above the line. The first inequality shows that y is less than or equal to $3x + 4$, so shade below the inequality. The graph of the solution of the first inequality looks like this:

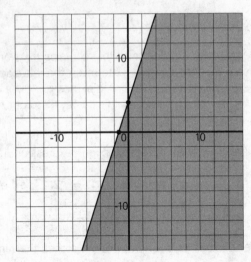

This is only shown in (B) and (C), so eliminate (A) and (D). The second inequality shows that y is less than or equal to $\frac{1}{4}x + 8$, so shade below the inequality. The graph of the solution of the second inequality looks like this:

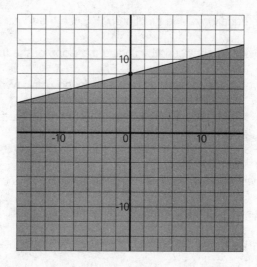

This is only shown in (C), which has the overlapping solutions to the two equations, so eliminate (B). The correct answer is (C).

16. **5** The question asks for the width of a three-dimensional shape given the volume, length, and height. The formula for volume of a rectangular solid is $V = lwh$, where V stands for volume, l stands for length, w stands for width, and h stands for height. Plug in the values that were given for the volume, length, and height to get $120 = (8)(w)(3) = 24w$. Divide both sides of the equation by 24 to get $5 = w$. The correct answer is 5.

18. **19** The question asks for the value of a function when given the graph of another function. The final question asks for the *value of function k when function j is at its minimum value*. To find the minimum of $j(x)$, look for the lowest point of the function in the given graph. The minimum of the graph has a value of $j(x)$ or $y = -2$. Plug this value for $j(x)$ into $k(x) = 17 - j(x)$ to get $k(x) = 17 - (-2) = 17 + 2 = 19$. The correct answer is 19.

20. **0** The question asks for the value of a function given a specific value of x. The question states that the function $q(x)$ is graphed in the given figure. The question also states that the function $n(x)$ is perpendicular to $q(x)$ and *passes through the point (2, –6)*. The equation of the function $n(x)$ is not given, so first find the equation of the function $n(x)$. Since the functions are perpendicular, the slope of the function $n(x)$ can be found by finding the slope of the function $q(x)$, and then taking the negative reciprocal. The slope of $q(x)$ can be found using two points from the line and the equation $slope = \dfrac{y_2 - y_1}{x_2 - x_1}$. Using the points (0, –10) and (5, 5), the equation becomes $slope = \dfrac{5 - (-10)}{5 - 0} = \dfrac{15}{5} = 3$. The slope can also be found by counting 3 up and 1 over, giving a slope of 3. The negative reciprocal of 3 is $-\dfrac{1}{3}$. The equation for $n(x)$ is $n(x) = -\dfrac{1}{3}x + b$, where b is the y–intercept. To find the y–intercept, plug the point (2, –6) into the equation and solve for b. The function becomes $-6 = -\dfrac{1}{3}(2) + b$. Simplify the right side of the equation to get $-6 = -\dfrac{2}{3} + b$. Add $\dfrac{2}{3}$ to both sides to get $-5\dfrac{1}{3} = b$, or $-\dfrac{16}{3} = b$. The final equation for $n(x)$ is $n(x) = -\dfrac{1}{3}x - \dfrac{16}{3}$. The question asks for *the value of n(–16)*. Plug $x = -16$ into the function, and solve for $n(x)$. The function becomes $n(-16) = -\dfrac{1}{3}(-16) - \dfrac{16}{3} = \dfrac{16}{3} - \dfrac{16}{3} = 0$. The correct answer is 0.

Math Calculator Explanations

2. **A** The question asks for a measurement and gives conflicting units. Start by ballparking. The question states that the *house had an estimated value of 600 drachmas*. Since *6 obols are equivalent to 1 drachma*, then the equivalent number of obols is going to be larger than the number of drachmas given. The only answer choice that is larger than the value of 600 drachmas is (A), 3,600. The correct answer is (A).

4. **D** The question asks for a value that is *NOT a solution to the equation*. Since the question asks

   for a specific value and the answers contain numbers in increasing order, plug in the answers.

   Begin by labeling the answer choices "x" and start with (B), -2. The equation becomes

   $\frac{1}{-2} = -\sqrt{\left(\frac{1}{-2}\right)^2}$ or $-\frac{1}{2} = -\sqrt{\frac{1}{4}}$. Take the square root on the right side of the equation to get

   $-\frac{1}{2} = -\frac{1}{2}$. Since both sides are equal, -2 *is* a solution to the equation, so eliminate (B). Try (C),

   -1 next. The equation becomes $\frac{1}{-1} = -\sqrt{\left(\frac{1}{-1}\right)^2}$ or $-1 = -\sqrt{\frac{1}{1}}$. Take the square root on the right

   side of the equation to get $-1 = -1$. Choice (C) is a solution, so eliminate (C). Plug in (D), 0, to

   get $\frac{1}{0} = -\sqrt{\left(\frac{1}{0}\right)^2}$. Dividing by 0 makes the fractions undefined, so 0 is *NOT* a solution to the

   equation. The correct answer is (D).

5. **A** The question asks for a certain value on a graph. The breaking point is defined as *where the material breaks and stress begins to decrease until it reaches zero*. On the graph, this would be the maximum value. The maximum value of the graph occurs at a time of 17 seconds. From this point, trace across to find the value of the *y*-coordinate. The value of the *y*-coordinate is 105 MPa. The correct answer is (A).

6. **D** The question asks for an interval with the least average rate of increase. Since rate of change on a graph is referred to as the slope, determine where the slope is increasing at the lowest rate. Look for where the curve is the least steep. On the graph, this occurs between 14 minutes and 16 minutes. The correct answer is (D).

7. **D** The question asks for the value of an angle on a figure. Start by labeling the figure with the given information. The value of x is given as 40, so label the angle as 40° on the figure. Since opposite angles are equal, label the angle opposite the 30° as 30°, and the angle opposite the 40° as 40°. The figure looks like this:

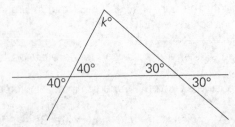

There are 180° in a triangle, so the value of k is 180° − 40° − 30° = 110°. The correct answer is (D).

9. **A** The question asks for a probability, which is defined as $\dfrac{\text{\# of outcomes that fit requirements}}{\text{total \# of outcomes}}$.

Read the table carefully to find the numbers to make the probability. The question asks for *the probability that an insect selected at random did not have spots*. The *# of outcomes that fit the requirements* is the number of insects that did not have spots, which is 30. The selection is taken from all of the insects, so the *total # of outcomes* is the total number of insects, or 73. Therefore, the probability is $\dfrac{30}{73}$. The correct answer is (A).

11. **B** The question asks for the length of Rope 3, *in feet*, which is related to the lengths of other ropes. Start with Process of Elimination. The question states that *the ratio of the lengths of Rope 1 to Rope 2 is the same as the ratio of the lengths of Rope 3 to Rope 4*. Since Rope 1 is shorter than Rope 2, Rope 3 must be shorter than Rope 4. Eliminate (D), which gives a length greater than Rope 4. Since there are equivalent ratios, set up a proportion. The proportion would be $\dfrac{\text{Rope 1}}{\text{Rope 2}} = \dfrac{\text{Rope 3}}{\text{Rope 4}}$. Fill in the lengths in the question, using x for the length of Rope 3, to

get $\dfrac{18}{27}=\dfrac{x}{54}$. Cross-multiply to get $972 = 27x$. Divide both sides by 27 to get $x = 36$ feet. The correct answer is (B).

13. **B** The question asks for the maximum number of 12-button jackets Steven can make given certain conditions. Since the question asks for a specific value and the answers contain numbers in increasing order, plug in the answers. The question states that *Steven needs to create at least 7 jackets.* The question also states that *he has no more than 75 buttons.* Begin by labeling the answers as "12-button jackets." Since the question asks for the maximum number of 12-button jackets he can make, start with (D), 7. If Steven makes 7 jackets with 12 buttons, he would use $7 \times 12 = 84$ buttons. This is more buttons than Steven has, so eliminate (D). Try (C), 5. If Steven makes 5 jackets with 12 buttons, he would use $5 \times 12 = 60$ buttons. For the 2 remaining 9-button jackets, he would use $2 \times 9 = 18$ buttons, for a total of $60 + 18 = 78$ buttons. This is still more than he has, so eliminate (C). Try (B), 4. For 4 jackets with 12 buttons, he would use $4 \times 12 = 48$ buttons. For the 3 remaining 9-button jackets, he would use $3 \times 9 = 27$ buttons, for a total of $48 + 27 = 75$ buttons. This matches the value given in the question. The correct answer is (B).

14. **A** The question asks for an equation to model a certain situation. Use Bite-Size Pieces and Process of Elimination to tackle this question. The question states that Sara's investment started with $90,000. Eliminate (D) because it doesn't include this term. The question says the stock *appreciated in value*, so an amount should be added to the initial investment. Eliminate (B), which subtracts from the initial amount. The question says the final value of the stock after 5 years was $165,000, but (C) multiplies $165,000 by y, meaning that amount was added every year. Eliminate (C). Since only one choice remains, it must be the correct one. It may be unclear where the number 15,000 came from, as it does not appear in the question. This is the result of dividing the total value increase of $75,000 by the number of years, which is 5. The correct answer is (A).

18. **D** The question asks for an equation that models a certain situation. Translate the information in Bite-Sized Pieces and eliminate after each piece. The question says *x percent of the magnesium required to complete the experiment is provided by y liters of solution S*. One piece of information says that *one liter of solution S* contains *20% of the full amount* of magnesium *required for Vivian's experiment*. The equation must contain $20y$, so eliminate (A), (B), and (C). The correct answer is (D).

19. **C** The question asks what volume of solution S is in one liter of the mixture. Since the question asks for a specific amount and the answers contain numbers in increasing order, plug in the answers. Begin by labeling the answers as "liters of solution S." First calculate the amount of salt contributed by one liter of solution S. The information states that $\frac{2}{3}$-*liter of solution S contains 120 grams of salt*. Set up a proportion to determine the amount of salt in one liter of solution S. The proportion is $\dfrac{\frac{2}{3}\text{-liter of solution S}}{120 \text{ grams of salt}} = \dfrac{1 \text{ liter of solution S}}{x \text{ grams of salt}}$. Cross-multiply to get $\frac{2}{3}x = 120$. To eliminate the $\frac{2}{3}$, multiply both sides by the reciprocal, which is $\frac{3}{2}$, to get $x = 180$ grams of salt. Start with (B), $\frac{1}{2}$ liter. A solution with a volume of $\frac{1}{2}$ liter of solution S would provide $\frac{1}{2} \times 180 = 90$ grams of salt. The remaining $\frac{1}{2}$ liter of solution T would provide $\frac{1}{2} \times 100 = 50$ grams of salt. The total grams of salt from both solutions is 90 + 50 = 140 grams. This does not match the value in the question, so eliminate (B). Since more salt is required in the solution, there needs to be a greater proportion of solution S, which has more salt per liter. Eliminate (A), which has a smaller proportion of solution S. Try (C), $\frac{3}{4}$ liter. A solution with a volume of $\frac{3}{4}$ liter solution S would provide $\frac{3}{4} \times 180 = 135$ grams of salt. The remaining $\frac{1}{4}$ liter of solution T would provide $\frac{1}{4} \times 100 = 25$ grams of salt. The total grams of salt from both solutions is 135 + 25 = 160 grams. This matches the value given in the question, so stop here. The correct answer is (C).

20. **D** The question asks for a graph that matches a given situation. Look at each graph carefully, and use Process of Elimination. The information says $\frac{2}{3}$-*liter of solution S contains 120 grams of salt*, so more solution S means more salt. The graph should be increasing, so eliminate (A) and

(B). Compare the remaining answer choices. Choices (C) and (D) have different y-intercepts.

No solution would mean no salt, so the y-intercept of the graph should be at the point $(0, 0)$.

Eliminate (C). The correct answer is (D).

23. **C**   The question asks for the reason a poll is not representative of *the entire population of the U.S.* Read each answer carefully and use Process of Elimination. Choice (A) refers to the distribution of "Yes" and "No" answers. It shouldn't necessarily be the case that the same percent of people would respond "No" as "Yes," so that's not a reason the poll is not representative. Eliminate (A). Choice (B) refers to the amount of time participants had to respond. The timing would not be a good reason to say the poll was not representative, so eliminate (B). Choice (C) asserts that the sample is not representative because it is not a *random sample*. This is true since the poll was taken only by readers of the magazine, who are likely dentists and whose opinions might not be representative of the entire U.S. population. Choice (D) mentions that the *percentages of respondents* don't add up to 100%, which is true, but is not an indication that not the poll is not representative, as the remaining 1% of respondents could have provided a different response or declined to answer. The correct answer is (C).

26. **A**   The question asks for the meaning of a *positive y-intercept, as depicted on a graph.* The y-intercept is the y-coordinate when the x-coordinate, in this case t, equals 0. The question states that m represents *the height of a ball in meters above the ground*, so the y-coordinate represents the height of the ball. Eliminate (C) and (D) which refer to a time. When $t = 0$ the ball is just being thrown, so it is at its initial height. The correct answer is (A).

29. **D**   The question asks which statement about *the decrease of the length of the icicle is supported by the line of best fit.* Use Process of Elimination, and get rid of answer choices that are not consistent with the graph and equation. The rate of change is the same as the slope of the line. The equation of the line is already in slope-intercept form, $y = mx + b$, where m represents the slope. In this case, the slope is -0.6. Eliminate (A) and (C), which don't use the slope as the rate of decrease. Compare the remaining answers. Choices (B) and (D) differ in the units used, either days or weeks. The x-axis is labeled as *Days since January* 5th, so the units of the x-axis are in days. Eliminate (B). The correct answer is (D).

31. **5**   The question asks for the radius of the circle based on two points on the circle which intersect the y-axis. Draw lines from the center of the circle to the two given points to create radii. The points are on the y-axis, so also draw a line from the center to the y-axis, perpendicular to the axis. The diagram will look like this:

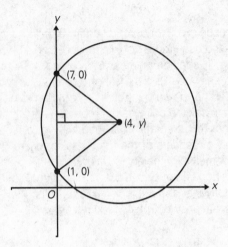

These lines, along with the y-axis itself, create two right triangles. The radii are the hypotenuses

of the triangles, so the Pythagorean Theorem can be used to determine their length. Because

of symmetry, the horizontal line drawn to the y-axis divides the line segment between (1, 0)

and (7, 0) in half. Its length is half of the total length of the segment, which is $\dfrac{7-1}{2} = \dfrac{6}{2} = 3$.

Therefore, the leg of each triangle that is on the y-axis has a length of 3. The length of the line

segment from the center of the circle to the y-axis is the x-coordinate of the center, which is 4.

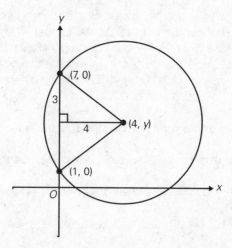

Note that this is a 3-4-5 right triangle, or use the Pythagorean theorem to calculate the length of the hypotenuse. The Pythagorean Theorem says that the sides of a right triangle are related by the equation $a^2 + b^2 = c^2$. Substituting the values for the sides of one of the right triangles gives $3^2 + 4^2 = c^2$. Simplifying this gives $9 + 16 = c^2$, or $25 = c^2$. Taking the square root of both sides gives $c = 5$. The correct answer is 5.

33. **40** The question asks for a probability, which is defined as $\dfrac{\text{\# of outcomes that fit requirements}}{\text{total \# of outcomes}}$.

Read the table carefully to find the numbers to make the probability. The question states that *if*

one blue shirt is selected at random, the probability that the size of the shirt is medium is $\dfrac{1}{4}$.

Since the question selects only from blue shirts, the total number of outcomes is $20 + 30 + 40$

$+ x + 30$, which is equal to $120 + x$. The desired outcome is a medium shirt, but it is selected

from the blue shirts only, so the number of desired outcomes is 40. The probability is then

$\dfrac{40}{120 + x}$. Set this equal to the probability in the question to get $\dfrac{40}{120 + x} = \dfrac{1}{4}$. Cross-multiply to

get $160 = 120 + x$. Subtract 120 from both sides to get $x = 40$. The correct answer is 40.

37. **1.05** The question asks for the difference, *to the nearest cent*, between the medians of two sets of numbers. The median of a list of numbers is the middle number when all values are arranged in order. Check carefully to note whether the lists are properly ordered. Both lists are already sorted from least to greatest, so the median of each is just the middle number. The median for Save-a-Lot is $20.40. The median for Good Deals is $21.45. The difference between the two is $21.45 – $20.40 = $1.05. The correct answer is 1.05.

38. **2** The question asks how many more dollars a blender costs at Save-a-Lot than at Low Cost Appliances. Translate the information in Bite-Sized Pieces. The question states that *at Save-a-Lot, the price of a blender was 7% less than at Low Cost Appliances department store*. Let S represent the Save-a-Lot price and L represent the Low Cost Appliances price. The equation becomes $S = L - 7\%(L)$. Substituting the amount from the table for Save-a-Lot gives $26.50 = L - 7\%(L)$. Percent means to divide by 100, so the equation becomes $26.50 = L - \dfrac{7}{100}L$. Multiply both sides by 100 to get $2,650 = 100L - 7L$, which simplifies to $2,650 = 93L$. Divide both sides by 93 to get $L = 28.49$. The question states that *the price of a blender was d dollars less at Save-a-Lot than at Low Cost Appliances*, or $S = L - d$. The equation becomes $26.50 = 28.49 - d$, so $d = 1.99. The question asks for the amount to the nearest dollar, or $2. The correct answer is 2.

STEP 3: Determine Your Goals

Now that you are a little more familiar with the structure and content of the SAT, let's discuss the specifics. The SAT always follows the same structure:

Test	Time (minutes)	Number of Questions
Reading	65	52
Writing and Language	35	44
Math (No Calculator)	25	20
Math (Calculator)	55	38

The 1600-point score is the sum of the two 800-point Area scores: Evidence-Based Reading and Writing (what we will simply call Verbal—it's the Reading section and the Writing and Language section together) and Math (both the non-calculator and calculator sections together). First, let's talk about how to use your total score to determine your target Verbal score and your target Math score. Let's say you are aiming for a total score of 1200, for instance. If on your practice test you did equally well on Math and Verbal, you might aim for a 600 on both Math and Verbal. On the other hand, if you scored higher on, say, Math, you might aim for a higher score on that section—perhaps a 500 on Verbal and a 700 on Math. Either way, your total score will be 1200.

> The College Board calls each section a "test" instead of a "section," but we'll use the terms interchangeably.

SAT Scoring

You should have a target total SAT score out of 1600 based on the research you have done (remember, your target score should be based on the average scores of the freshman class at the schools you are considering applying to). You should also have a starting score from your first practice test. Now we are going to show you how to use those two scores to determine your goal for each section of the SAT.

When thinking about your two Area scores, you may want to consider which area you enjoy working on or which area has skills that are easiest for you to improve upon. For example, maybe you scored equally well on the two areas on the practice test, but you hate Math and only want to work on your Verbal score. In that case, try setting your Verbal goal higher. It's all up to you! Just keep in mind that there is no reason you need to do equally well on both areas. One other note is that while colleges are most interested in your overall score out of 1600, as we mentioned in Step 2, some programs may have specific requirements or parts of the score that they emphasize. That information may also guide your Area score goals.

Once you have determined your Verbal and Math goals, it's time to get more specific and take a look at the contents of each Area. Although the Math has two sections (calculator and non-calculator), the two sections contain roughly the same content, so there is no reason to create separate calculator and non-calculator goals. However, the Verbal section is a different story. Just like we said above, your Verbal score is a combination of your Reading score and your Writing and Language score. That might seem odd because those two sections test completely different skills: Reading tests your ability to comprehend and answer questions about a text, whereas Writing and Language tests grammar, punctuation, and consistency within a text. Some people do equally well with these two sets of tasks, but many people are stronger in one than the other. Can you guess where we're going with this? Just as you balanced the Math and Verbal scores to reflect your strengths, you can balance the Reading score and Writing and Language score in the same way. Let's take a look at how those two scores come together.

On your score report for either a practice test or a real SAT, you will find a section that includes three "Test" scores. These scores range from 10–40 and are in the areas of Reading, Writing and Language, and Math. You don't really need to look at the Math Test score because it is just another form of your 800-point Math score: simply multiply the Math Test score by 20 and you'll have the Math Area score in a range from 200–800. However, the two separate Verbal Test scores are extremely useful. Here's how to calculate the 800-point Verbal score: add the Reading Test score and Writing and Language Test score together, then multiply the sum by 10. So, for example, if you scored a 30 on Reading and a 32 on Writing and Language, you would add them together (62) and multiply by 10 to get a Verbal score of 620.

You can work backwards from this scoring system to determine a target score for each of the two Verbal sections. Here is a worksheet to help you do that.

Target Verbal score (out of 800): _____

Cross off the last zero
and circle this number: _____

Your Reading Test and Writing and Language Test scores must add to the circled number. Use your practice test score report to decide what path you should take: do you want to aim for the same score in each of the two Verbal sections or aim higher in one section (if you are stronger in one)? Also, consider which one you think you can improve on more. It's important to note that the 10–40 Test score does not correspond to the exact number of questions you need to get right—in Step 4, you'll find out how many correct answers you need in order to achieve your target score in each section.

Your Target Scores

Reading: _____ out of 40

Writing and Language: _____ out of 40

Math: _____ out of 800

Let's take a look at some examples to see how different students might achieve the same score.

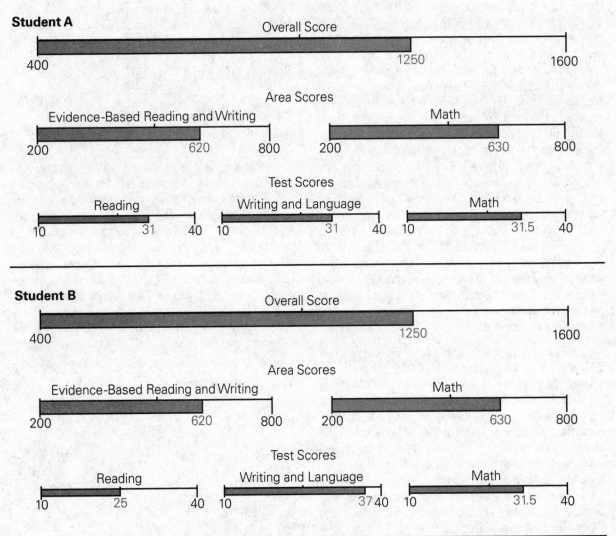

Student A

Overall Score

400 — 1250 — 1600

Area Scores

Evidence-Based Reading and Writing
200 — 620 — 800

Math
200 — 630 — 800

Test Scores

Reading
10 — 31 — 40

Writing and Language
10 — 31 — 40

Math
10 — 31.5 — 40

Student B

Overall Score

400 — 1250 — 1600

Area Scores

Evidence-Based Reading and Writing
200 — 620 — 800

Math
200 — 630 — 800

Test Scores

Reading
10 — 25 — 40

Writing and Language
10 — 37 40

Math
10 — 31.5 — 40

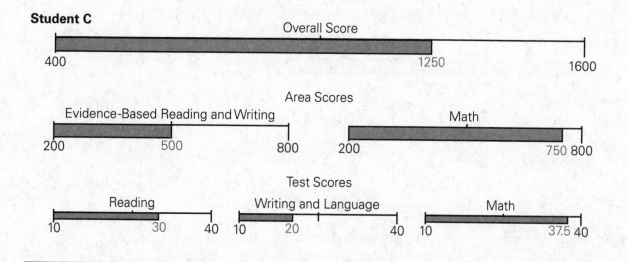

Student C

Overall Score
400 — 1250 — 1600

Area Scores

Evidence-Based Reading and Writing
200 — 500 — 800

Math
200 — 750 800

Test Scores

Reading
10 — 30 — 40

Writing and Language
10 — 20 — 40

Math
10 — 37.5 40

Notice that students A and B had the same Area scores, but student A scored equally well on Reading and on Writing and Language. Student B was much stronger in Writing and Language, so that balanced out a weaker Reading score. Student C achieved the same overall score as students A and B (1250) but had a very high Math score that balanced out a lower verbal score.

The above example demonstrates why it is not enough to only have a target overall score—having section goals will help you to determine where to put in your efforts for improvement. Take a look at your practice test: if you scored about the same in each area, then you may decide your goal is about the same on each section, unless there are some areas you think will be easier to improve than others. On the other hand, if you have a stronger area, lean into it! You don't just have to plan to improve your weaker areas to match the scores in your stronger areas. In

fact, you may find that your stronger area is easier to improve than your weaker area is—if you already do well on a section, you may only have a few small things to work on, and (bonus!) you may enjoy working on that subject more since it's one you excel at. The bottom line: make goals that will work for you.

In the next chapter, we'll discuss how many more questions you need to get correct to achieve your target scores.

STEP 4: Make Your Goals Specific

In Step 3, you determined your goal score for each section of the SAT. Now that you know what *scores* you're aiming for, let's talk about how many more *questions* you need to get correct to achieve those scores.

On the next few pages, you'll find some scoring charts that show how the number of correct answers corresponds to the test score for Reading, Writing and Language, and Math, respectively. (The number of questions that corresponds to a certain score on the SAT varies a little from test to test, but these charts will give you a good basis for setting your goals.)

Look up your goal score for each test, then read across the row to find the number of questions you need to get correct.

Verbal Score Calculation

Verbal Score = (Reading Scale Score + Writing and Language Scale Score) × 10

For a Reading *Test Score* of:	You need about this many *Correct Answers:*
10	<3
12	5
14	7
16	10
18	14
20	18
22	21
24	26
26	29
28	33
30	37
32	41
34	44
36	47
38	50
40	52

For a Writing and Language *Test Score* of:	You need about this many *Correct Answers:*
10	3
12	5
14	8
16	10
18	13
20	16
22	19
24	22
26	25
28	28
30	31
32	34
34	37
36	40
38	42
40	44

For a Math *Test Score* of:	You need about this many *Correct Answers:*
350	12
400	16
450	20
500	26
550	32
600	39
650	44
700	50
750	54
800	58

For illustration, let's imagine a student—we'll call him Joe Bloggs. Joe's total score goal is 1300. In order to achieve this goal, Joe Bloggs has set the following goals for his area scores:

Evidence-Based Reading and Writing: 550
Math: 650

To get a 550 in Evidence-Based Reading and Writing, Joe has decided to aim for a Writing and Language score of 30 and a Reading score of 25.

To get a score of 25 on the Reading Test, Joe needs to get 27–28 questions correct.

To get a score of 30 on the Writing and Language Test, he needs to get 31 questions correct.

To get a Math area score of 650, he needs to get a total of 44 questions correct (including both the "No Calculator" and "Calculator" sections).

How many questions do you need to get correct on each section to reach your goal scores?

Reading: _____

Writing and Language: _____

Math: _____

If you took the Free SAT Practice Test on the Princeton Review website, log into your account and open the score report from your test. As you click on the tab for each area score—Verbal and Math— you will see how many questions you got correct, how many questions you got wrong, and how many questions you left blank.

Next, determine how many *more* correct answers you need in each section to achieve your goal scores. Compare the number of correct answers you need to the number of correct answers you got on your practice test.

Let's see what this looks like for Joe. On his first practice test, Joe got the following:

23 questions correct in Reading
26 questions correct in Writing and Language
34 questions correct in Math

In order to achieve his goal scores, Joe needs the following:

4–5 more questions correct in Reading

5 more questions correct in Writing and Language

10 more questions correct in Math (total for both Math sections)

How many more questions do you need to get correct?

Reading: _____

Writing and Language: _____

Math: _____

As you can see, getting just a handful more questions correct can raise your SAT score significantly! In the next chapter, you'll make a plan for how to get those extra questions correct.

STEP 5: Make a Plan

Now that you know how many more questions you need to get correct in each section, let's make a plan for how to focus your preparation.

There are two key ways to improve your accuracy on a test like the SAT. The first is to adjust your test-taking strategies. The second is to work on content and skills for specific sections or types of questions.

If you were going to devote your whole life to studying for the SAT, you could learn all of the content and skills for all of the questions in all four sections of the test. But we sincerely hope that is not your plan. After all, you have plenty of other things on your plate and better things to do! So, your mission is to design an efficient plan that focuses on a few areas that will have a significant impact on your score. How will you do that?

Begin with Test-Taking Strategies

First, hone your skills for the SAT as a whole. Get to know the structure of the test and how it is scored. Learn strategies that maximize your score on the SAT—a standardized, timed, multiple-choice test. No matter your areas of strength or weakness, you will benefit from becoming a savvy test-taker.

> Use Step 6 to learn the strategies you need for the SAT as a whole.

Maximize your Strengths

The best way to improve your score is to shore up your weaknesses while exploiting your strengths as much as possible. To this end, remember the following:

> To lift your score as high as possible, maximize your performance on your strongest topics.

You don't need to be a rock star on every topic that appears on the test. Identify a few types of questions on each section that you feel good about and maximize your performance on those questions. Are you strongest at Writing and Language questions about punctuation, Reading passages about science topics, and Math questions about algebra? Then work to raise your accuracy on those questions as high as you can. You shouldn't ignore your weaknesses, but recognize that the work you put in on your strengths will yield greater dividends. Think of it this way: if you had only one hour to devote to practice the week before the SAT, you would put that hour toward your best subjects.

It's also a good idea to focus first on the topics and types of questions that appear often on the test, since those have the biggest impact on your score.

> Use Step 7 to learn the skills and strategies for the Reading, Writing and Language, and Math Tests.

Determine your Strengths and Weaknesses

In order to maximize your strengths, you must know your strengths! If you took the Princeton Review's free SAT practice test, you can easily use the score report from your practice test to get to know your strengths and weaknesses.

Remember Joe Bloggs? Let's take a look at the Reading section of the score report from his first practice test.

1. Reading

✓ 23 Correct ✗ 25 Incorrect ◯ 4 Unanswered

1 ✗	2 ✗	3 ✓	4 ✗	5 ✗	6 ✓	7 ✗	8 ✓	9 ✗	10 ✓
11 ✓	12 ✗	13 ✓	14 ✗	15 ✗	16 ✓	17 ✓	18 ✓	19 ✓	20 ✓
21 ✓	22 ✓	23 ✗	24 ✓	25 ✓	26 ✗	27 ✗	28 ✓	29 ✗	30 ✓
31 ✓	32 ✗	33 ✓	34 ✗	35 ✗	36 ✗	37 ✗	38 ✗	39 ✗	40 ✗
41 ✗	42 ✗	43 ✓	44 ✗	45 ✓	46 ✓	47 ✗	48 ✓		

◯ 49 ◯ 50 ◯ 51 ◯ 52

This is the "Section" view of Joe's Reading Test. Questions with a check mark are correct, questions with a "x" are incorrect, and circled questions were left blank. What can you learn from this view?

You can see that Joe ran out of time at the end of the test—he left questions 49 through 52 blank. Questions 1–10 belong to the first passage, 11–21 belong to the second passage, 22–31 belong to the third passage, 32–41 belong to the fourth passage, and 42–52 belong to the fifth passage. You can see that Joe did better on some passages than others—for example, he got 8 questions correct on the second passage, but only 4 questions correct on the first passage. On the last passage—the one where he ran out of time—Joe got four of the questions he answered correct, so his accuracy was as good on that passage as it was on the first passage, even though he only worked half the questions!

The takeaway: Joe should adjust his approach to use his time more effectively. He should pay attention to the "Pacing," "Personal Order of Difficulty," and "Guessing" strategies in Step 6. He should also focus on the pacing and order of difficulty information in the Reading section of Step 7.

Next, let's view Joe's Reading score report by "Category."

If you don't have a Princeton Review score report, you can make a chart for yourself and mark which questions you got right, got wrong, or skipped entirely in each section. Then you can try to identify these patterns on your own. You should do this for each of the four sections of the test.

In this chapter, we mention the names of some strategies—such as Personal Order of Difficulty--that are covered in Steps 6 and 7. Don't worry that you don't know what the strategies are yet. You'll be familiar with them soon.

Reading Responses by Category

✓23 Correct ✗25 Incorrect ○4 Unanswered

Explicit Meanings 5/7	Implicit Meanings 2/4	Analogical reasoning 0/1
✓8 ✓11 ✓17 ✓28 ✓46	✓30 ✓48 ✗26 ✗35	✗5
✗14 ✗32		

Citing Textual Evidence 1/10	Central Ideas & Themes 1/2	Summarizing 0/1
✓18 ✗2 ✗9 ✗15 ✗27	✓22 ✗42	✗12
✗29 ✗37 ✗39 ✗44 ✗47		

Vocabulary in Context 6/8	Analyzing Word Choice 1/1	Overall Text Structure 1/1
✓3 ✓6 ✓13 ✓16 ✓25	✓24	✓43
✓33 ✗7 ✗34		

Part-Whole Relationships 2/3	Point of View 1/3	Purpose 0/1
✓31 ✓45 ✗4	✓10 ✗1 ✗23	✗41

Claims & Counterclaims 0/1	Reasoning 0/1	Multiple Texts 0/2
○49	✗36	✗38 ✗40

Quantitative Information 3/6		
✓19 ✓20 ✓21 ○50 ○51		
○52		

What can you learn from this view?

Joe has several areas of strength on the Reading Test. He did well with Explicit Meanings and Vocabulary in Context questions. He got all of the Quantitative Information questions that he answered correct, but he left three of the questions in that category blank.

The takeaway: Joe should be sure to answer all of the questions of the types he is best at. He should also focus on maximizing his accuracy on those types of questions. He's already good at them, and there are lots of them, so if he can identify what went wrong with the few questions he missed and correct those errors, he'll boost his score significantly.

If Joe had answered all of the Quantitative Information questions correctly, and gotten just one more Explicit Meanings and one more Vocabulary in Context question correct, how would he do? He would have gotten a total of 5 more questions correct. If you look back at Step 4, you'll see that Joe's goal was to get 4–5 more questions correct in the Reading Test. So, by focusing on basic strategy and on his areas of strength, Joe can reach his goal.

Finally, you can see that Joe found some of the other question types more challenging—for example, he missed most of the Citing Textual Evidence questions, half of the Implicit Meanings questions, and both of the Multiple Texts questions. Once Joe has maximized his score in his areas of strength, he could work on strategies for those types of questions. Of the remaining question types, Citing Textual Evidence would be a good one to focus on since there are so many of those questions.

> **If you don't have a Princeton Review score report with this category view, use these Reading categories to classify the questions on the test you took. Figuring out what each question tests is good practice to help you identify question types, and it will allow you to see your strengths and weaknesses more clearly. Repeat the process for the other sections of the test.**

Next, let's take a look at Joe's Writing and Language Test.

2. Writing and Language

✓ 26 Correct ✗ 15 Incorrect ◯ 3 Unanswered

✓ 1	✓ 2	✓ 3	✓ 4	✗ 5	✗ 6	✓ 7	✗ 8	✓ 9	✓ 10
✗ 11	✗ 12	✓ 13	✓ 14	✓ 15	✓ 16	✗ 17	✓ 18	✓ 19	✗ 20
✗ 21	✓ 22	✓ 23	✓ 24	✗ 25	✓ 26	✓ 27	✗ 28	✓ 29	✓ 30
✗ 31	✓ 32	✗ 33	✓ 34	✗ 35	✓ 36	✓ 37	✓ 38	✗ 39	✗ 40
✓ 41	◯ 42	◯ 43	◯ 44						

This is the "Section" view of Joe's Writing and Language Test. What can you learn from this view?

You can see that Joe ran out of time at the end of the test—he left questions 42 through 44 blank.

The takeaway: Joe should adjust his approach to use his time more effectively. He should pay attention to the "Pacing," "Personal Order of Difficulty," and "Guessing" strategies in Step 6. He should also focus on the pacing and order of difficulty information in the Writing and Language section of Step 7.

Next, let's view Joe's Writing and Language score report by "Category."

Writing and Language Responses by Category

✓ 26 Correct ✗ 15 Incorrect ○ 3 Unanswered

Proposition	0/1	Supporting an Argument	2/3	Focus	1/4
✗ 33		✓ 1 ✓ 41 ✗ 20		✓ 26 ✗ 6 ✗ 17 ✗ 40	

Quantitative Information	1/1	Sentence Ordering	0/2	Introductions, Conclusions, Transitions	3/5
✓ 29		✗ 31 ✗ 39		✓ 15 ✓ 18 ✓ 36 ✗ 5 ✗ 8	

Precision	3/4	Concision	0/4	Syntax	1/1
✓ 4 ✓ 19 ✓ 26 ○ 42		✗ 11 ✗ 21 ○ 43 ○ 44		✓ 9	

Sentence Construction	3/3	Connecting Complete Sentences	2/2	Verbs	2/3
✓ 7 ✓ 16 ✓ 37		✓ 24 ✓ 27		✓ 10 ✓ 14 ✗ 35	

Understanding Pronoun Ambiguity	1/1	Adjectives vs. Adverbs	2/2	Subject Verb Agreement	1/1
✓ 2		✓ 22 ✓ 30		✓ 32	

Noun Agreement	1/1	Faulty Comparison	0/1	Idioms	0/1
✓ 34		✗ 12		✗ 25	

Within-Sentence Punctuation	1/2	Nonrestrictive Elements	2/2		
✓ 13 ✗ 28		✓ 3 ✓ 38			

What can you learn from this view?

Joe has several areas of strength on the Writing and Language Test. For example, he got all of the questions correct in the categories Sentence Construction, Connecting Complete Sentences, and Nonrestrictive Elements. These categories are related to punctuation and joining complete and incomplete ideas correctly. Joe got half of the Within-Sentence Punctuation questions correct. Joe should focus on those types of questions—he's already good at them, so he should identify what went wrong with the one question he missed and correct that error, and make sure he feels confident about the punctuation rules.

Joe also did well with questions about Verbs, Pronouns, Nouns, and Adjectives/Adverbs. Joe should focus on those types of questions—he's already good at them, so he should identify what went wrong with the one question he missed and correct that error, and make sure he feels confident about the most frequently-tested rules about verbs, pronouns, nouns, and adjectives/adverbs.

Joe also did well on the Quantitative Information question (just as he did on the Reading Test).

Joe had more trouble with the questions in the Proposition, Supporting an Argument, Focus, Sentence Ordering, and Introductions, Conclusions, and Transitions categories. When he looks back at this test, Joe will see that these questions look different from many of the other questions—they all start with an actual question. To shore up this weaker area, Joe should learn the basic approach for this style of question.

Finally, Joe had trouble with Concision questions. Joe should learn about what the College Board is testing in these questions, so he has a better idea of what to focus on.

Notice that questions on Idioms and Faulty Comparison don't come up very often, so these will not have a big effect on Joe's score. Since they were tough for him and don't appear very often, these might be good "Letter of the Day" questions for Joe.

If Joe had answered all of the questions in his areas of strength correctly, guessed his Letter of the Day for the questions he left blank, and gotten just a couple of additional questions correct from the categories he finds most challenging, he could easily answer five more questions correctly. If you look back at Step 4, you'll see that Joe's goal was to get 5 more questions correct in the Writing and Language Test.

> **You'll learn more about the Letter of the Day in Step 6.**

Next, let's take a look at Joe's Math Test.

3. Math (No Calculator)

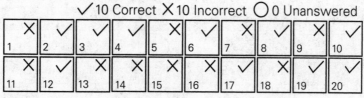

4. Math (With Calculator)

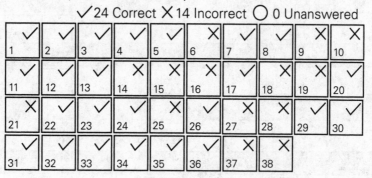

This is the view of Joe's Math Test by section. What can you learn from this view?

You can see that Joe answered all 58 of the Math questions and got 34 of them correct.

In the No Calculator section, questions 1–15 are multiple-choice, and questions 16–20 are "grid-in" questions. In the Calculator section, questions 1–30 are multiple-choice, and questions 31–38 are "grid-in" questions. The questions of each type are arranged in a rough order of difficulty, with easier multiple-choice questions followed by harder multiple-choice

questions, and then easier grid-in questions followed by tougher grid-in questions. You can see that Joe missed some of the easier questions near the beginning of each section. There is a good chance that he made some careless errors because he was rushing to work all on all of the questions.

The takeaway: Joe should adjust his approach to use his time more effectively. He should pay attention to the "Pacing," "Personal Order of Difficulty," and "Guessing" strategies in Step 6. He should also focus on the pacing and order of difficulty information in the Math section of Step 7.

Next let's look at Joe's Math score by category.

Math Responses by Category

✓ 34 Correct ✗ 24 Incorrect ◯ 0 Unanswered

Tackling Linear Equations 5/5	Tackling Linear Inequalities 2/2	Building Functions 1/2	Two-Variable Linear Inequalities 0/1
✓3 ✓3 ✓4 ✓8 ✓17	✓17 ✓20	✓1 ✗11	✗25
Two-Variable Linear Equations 2/2	Translating Functions 1/1	Translating Functions & their Graphs 0/3	Conversions 3/3
✓2 ✓20	✓31	✗9 ✗9 ✗16	✓12 ✓32 ✓36
Percentages 1/1	Scatterplots 3/3	Graphs Highlights 1/1	Linear vs. Exponential Growth 0/5
✓22	✓11 ✓13 ✓26	✓23	✗14 ✗15 ✗18 ✗37 ✗38
Interpreting Tables 2/2	Summarizing Population Data 1/1	Analyzing Population Data 2/2	Comparing Expressions with Structure 2/2
✓7 ✓8	✓5	✓24 ✓30	✓6 ✓29
Solving Quadratic Equations 0/1	Working with Polynomials 0/1	Solving Radical & Rational Equations 1/2	Solving Systems of Equations 1/1
✗13	✗27	✓12 ✗7	✓10
Simplifying Rational Expressions 1/1	Sketching Graphs 0/1	Nonlinear 2-Variable Relationships 0/2	Interpreting Functions 0/2
✓4	✗10	✗14 ✗28	✗1 ✗5
Breaking Down Equations 2/2	Solving Volume Problems 0/1	Right triangle Rules 0/1	Working with Imaginary Numbers 0/1
✓19 ✓33	✗19	✗16	✗15
Calculating Circle Properties 1/2	Congruence & Similarity Problems 0/1	Tackling Rates 2/3	
✓35 ✗21	✗18	✓2 ✓34 ✗6	

What can you learn from this view?

Joe did particularly well on questions that involve interpreting tables and graphs, including Scatterplots and Interpreting Tables. He also did well on arithmetic topics, including Percentages, Conversions, and Tackling Rates. He did miss one problem on Rates early in the section.

This category view combines all Math questions from sections 3 and 4, which is why some categories (such as Tackling Linear Equations) have two entries with the same question number.

The takeaway: Joe should seek out the questions on tables and graphs, as well as the arithmetic topics he feels confident about. If he focuses on those questions and works them carefully, he can avoid careless errors and maximize his score on these topics.

Joe had a little more trouble with algebra topics (for example, categories involving Functions and Nonlinear equations), but he still got many of these problems correct (for example, questions about Linear Equations and Inequalities). There are lots of questions in these categories, so they will have a big impact on Joe's score.

The takeaway: algebra would be a productive area for Joe to focus on. He's got a good foundation, and he just needs a brush up on some topics, along with strategies for tackling the tougher algebra problems.

Geometry was tougher for Joe. He missed several questions in the Right Triangle Rules, Solving Volume Problems, Calculating Circle Properties, and Congruence and Similarity Problems categories. However, there are not as many of these questions.

The takeaway: Joe could work on Process of Elimination strategies for geometry questions to help him guess correctly more often. If he has time, he could also brush up on basic geometry formulas and work on his strategy for tackling geometry questions. When he's taking the test, he shouldn't spend time slogging through tough geometry problems until he has answered all the questions on which he feels more confident.

If Joe could answer 3–4 more of the algebra questions correctly, eliminate 4–5 careless mistakes, and use Process of Elimination to guess correctly on 1–2 tougher questions, he could achieve his goal of getting 10 more questions correct in the Math Test. So, by focusing on basic strategy and on his areas of strength, Joe can reach his goal.

Your Turn

Now, look at your own score report from your practice test. Look at both the "Section" and "Category" views for each section. Did you run out of time or rush through any section? Did you spend a long time on a very difficult problem, when you could have spent the time on easier questions? Which types of questions were you best at? Which topics did you struggle with?

Look back at your goals in Step 4. How many more questions do you need to get correct in each section? Which questions should you focus on to accomplish your goals? Make notes about which topics will be best for you to focus on during your preparation. Focus on maximizing your performance in your strong areas, and seek out strategies to minimize missed questions in your weaker areas. Start with the most frequently-tested question types, since these will have the biggest impact on your score.

Grab a notebook or some scratch paper to make your notes about your strengths and weaknesses and what you will focus on during your preparation.

Planning your Preparation Time

How will you fit in the study you need to do? Sit down with a calendar and map out the time you have between now and the date you will take the SAT. If you haven't decided when to take the test yet, making that decision is a good first step in your planning.

Think about how much time you have during the week to work on the SAT. It's more effective to study for a short time on several days during the week than to do a mega-session every once in a while. If you have several weeks or months before the SAT, you can set aside some days to take additional practice tests (you'll find sources for additional practice tests in Step 8). It's also important not to burn yourself out, so give yourself breaks, and leave time to eat, sleep, exercise, and relax!

What follows is a sample plan for a student who has five weeks before the SAT. This plan includes three or four study sessions per week. You can use this is a template, adjusting as you need for your schedule. If you have more time, you can supplement your practice with other resources—see Step 8 for ideas.

Week 1 (You may have already completed these sessions!)

Session One: Take the first practice test and score it.

Session Two: Review your score report and set your goals, using Step 4 as a guide.

Session Three: Review your score report and decide what areas to focus on, using Step 5 as a guide.

Week 2

Session Four: Read through Step 6, noting the shifts in strategy that will help you improve your accuracy and efficiency on all sections of the SAT.

Session Five: Read through the strategies for Reading in Step 7. Practice these strategies using a timed Reading section from one of the additional sources described in Step 8.

Session Six: Review your work on the timed Reading section. Which strategies did you apply well? How could you improve your accuracy and efficiency?

Week 3

Session Seven: Read through the strategies for Writing and Language in Step 7. Practice these strategies using a timed Writing and Language section from one of the additional sources described in Step 8.

Session Eight: Review your work on the timed Writing and Language section. Which strategies did you apply well? How could you improve your accuracy and efficiency?

Session Nine: Read through the strategies for Math in Step 7. Practice these strategies using a timed "No Calculator" Math section from one of the additional sources described in Step 8.

Week 4

Session Ten: Review your work on the timed "No Calculator" Math section. Which strategies did you apply well? How could you improve your accuracy and efficiency?

Session Eleven: Practice the Math strategies using a timed "Calculator" Math section from one of the additional sources described in Step 8.

Session Twelve: Review your work on the timed "Calculator" Math section. Which strategies did you apply well? How could you improve your accuracy and efficiency?

Week 5

Session Thirteen: Take a full practice test. Use the techniques you've been learning and practicing for each section.

Session Fourteen: Score your test and go through the explanations for Reading and Writing and Language. Focus on where you may have missed the opportunity to use a technique and on your decisions about which questions to attempt, given your pacing goals and Personal Order of Difficulty.

> Look for the Personal Order of Difficulty strategy in Step 6.

Session Fifteen: Go through the explanations for the two Math sections. Focus on where you may have missed the opportunity to use a technique and on your decisions about which questions to attempt, given your pacing goals and Personal Order of Difficulty.

Session Sixteen: Review your pacing goals and major strategies for each section of the test. Do something fun and relaxing to de-stress before the test!

Grab a notebook, a calendar, or another way to plan your preparation and put it down in writing!

Now you have your plan in place. In the next chapter, we'll learn the strategies that apply to all sections of test.

STEP 6: Learn Big Picture Strategies

Now that you have a plan about how to focus your time, let's look at the strategies that will improve your accuracy and efficiency on both the Math and the Evidence-Based Reading and Writing sections of the SAT.

The Basic Approach

The SAT test is different from the tests you take in school, so you need to approach it differently. To be effective, SAT strategies have to be based on the SAT and not on any other test. You need to know how the SAT is scored and how it's constructed.

Scoring

You've already seen that you get a "test score" for each section of the SAT, and that the test score is based on the "raw score"—the number of questions you get correct. There are a few other important details to consider about the way the SAT is scored.

How many raw points is an easy question worth? How many raw points is a difficult question worth? An easy question is worth 1 raw point, and a difficult question is also worth 1 raw point. So, you don't get any more credit for working a hard question than you do for working an easy question.

How many points is a blank answer worth? If you guessed 0, you're right. But what about a wrong answer—do you lose points when you answer incorrectly? Nope! A wrong answer is also worth 0 points.

Structure

Let's review the structure of the SAT. The four sections are always given in the same order. (You may be asked to complete a short experimental section, where the College Board tests out new questions, but it doesn't count toward your score, so we're not going to worry about it.)

	Amount of Time	# of Questions
Reading	65 minutes	52 questions
Writing and Language	35 minutes	44 questions
Math (No Calculator)	25 minutes	20 questions
Math (Calculator)	55 minutes	38 questions

ENEMY #1: TIME

How much time do you have per question on the Calculator section of the Math Test? You have just under a minute and a half, and that's generous compared with the time given per question on the other sections. How often do you take a test in school with about a minute per question? If you do at all, it's maybe on a quiz but probably not on a major exam or final. Time is your enemy on the SAT, and you have to use it wisely and be aware of how that time pressure can bring out your worst instincts as a test-taker.

ENEMY #2: YOURSELF

Many people struggle with test anxiety in school and on standardized tests. But there is something particularly evil about tests like the SAT and ACT. The skills you've been rewarded for throughout your academic career can easily work against you on the SAT. You've been taught since birth to follow directions, go in order, and finish everything. But that approach won't necessarily earn you your highest SAT score.

On the other hand, treating the SAT as a scary, alien beast can leave your brain blank and useless and can incite irrational, self-defeating behavior. When you pick up a No. 2 pencil, you may tend to leave your common sense at the door. Test nerves and anxieties can make you misread a question, commit a careless error, see something that isn't there, blind you to what is there, talk you into a bad answer, and worst of all, convince you to spend good time on "bad" questions.

There is good news. You can—and will—crack the SAT. You will learn how to approach it differently than you would a test in school, and you won't let the test crack you. The structure and the scoring of the test shape the best strategies for the SAT.

Be warned that some of the approaches we're going to show you may seem counterintuitive or unnatural. Some of these strategies may be very different from the way you learned to approach similar questions in school, but trust us! Try tackling the questions using our techniques, and keep practicing until they become easier. When you do this, you'll see a real improvement in your score.

SAT Strategies

Personal Order of Difficulty (POOD)

If time is going to run out, would you rather it run out on the hardest questions or the easiest? You know that hard questions are not worth any more than easy questions, so of course, you want time to run out on the questions you are less likely to get right.

You can easily fall into the trap of spending too much time on the hardest problems and either never getting to or rushing through the easiest (Remember Joe's test from Step 5?). You shouldn't work in the order the College Board provides just because it's in that order. Instead, find your own Personal Order of Difficulty (POOD). Make smart decisions about which questions you'll do Now, Later, and Never as you move through each test. Make your decisions quickly and for good reasons.

Now

Do you know how to do the question? Can you do it fairly quickly and accurately? Do it *Now*.

Later

Will this question take more time to work, but you still think you know how to do it? Leave it and come back to it *Later*. Circle the question number so you can find it easily when you come back.

Never

Test-taker, know thyself. Know the topics that are your worst, and learn the signs that flash danger. Don't waste time on questions you should *Never* do. Instead, use more time to answer the Now and Later questions accurately.

Pacing

The SAT may be designed so that you run out of time, but you can't rush through it as fast as possible. All you'll do is make careless errors on easy questions you should get right and spend way too much time on difficult ones you're unlikely to get right (like Joe did!). Let your POOD help determine your pacing. Go slowly enough to answer all the Now questions correctly but quickly enough to get to the number of Later questions you need to reach your goal score.

In Step 4, you identified the number of questions you need to reach your goal score in each section. Practice your pacing on practice tests (see Step 8 for additional practice resources), going slowly enough to avoid careless errors and quickly enough to reach your goal scores.

Slow down, score more. You're not scored on **how many questions you do**. You're scored on **how many questions you answer correctly**. Doing fewer questions can mean more correct answers overall!

Process of Elimination (POE)

Multiple-choice tests offer one great advantage: they provide the correct answer right there on the page. Of course, they hide the correct answer among three incorrect answers. It's often easier to spot the wrong answers than it is to identify the right ones, particularly when you apply a smart Process of Elimination (POE). As you work each question, actively look for answers that are wrong and physically cross them off on the page. This will help you avoid traps and make a better guess if you need to.

POE works differently on each section of the SAT, but it's a powerful strategy on all of them. For some question types, you'll always use POE rather than wasting time trying to figure out the answer on your own. For other questions, you'll use POE when you're stuck. The College Board hides the correct answer among wrong ones, but when you cross off just one or two wrong answers, the correct answer can become

more obvious, sometimes jumping right off the page. Try this example.

What's the capital of Azerbaijan?

Give up?

Unless you spend your spare time studying an atlas, you may not even know that Azerbaijan is a real country, much less what its capital is. If this question came up on a test, you'd have to skip it, wouldn't you? Well, maybe not. Let's turn this question into a multiple-choice question—just like the majority of questions on the SAT.

1

What is the capital of Azerbaijan?

A) Washington, D.C.

B) Paris

C) London

D) Baku

The question doesn't seem that hard anymore, does it? Of course, we made our example extremely easy. (By the way, the SAT won't actually test your geography knowledge.)

But you'd be surprised by how many people give up on SAT questions that aren't much more difficult than this one just because they don't know the correct answer right off the top of their heads. "Capital of Azerbaijan? Oh, no! I've never heard of Azerbaijan!"

These students don't stop to think that they might be able to find the correct answer simply by eliminating all of the answer choices they know are wrong. Wrong answers are usually easier to find than the right ones are. After all, there are more of them! Remember the question about Azerbaijan? Even though you didn't know the answer off the top of your head, you easily figured it out by eliminating the three obviously incorrect choices. You looked for wrong answers first.

It's Not About Circling the Right Answer

Physically marking in your test booklet what you think of certain answers can help you narrow down choices, take the best possible guess, and save time!

Try using the following notations:

✔   Put a check mark next to an answer you like.

~   Put a squiggle next to an answer you kind of like.

?   Put a question mark next to an answer you don't understand.

A)   Cross out the letter of any answer choice you KNOW is wrong.

You can always come up with your own system, and you may not need all these categories for every section of the test.

There won't be many questions on the SAT in which incorrect choices will be as easy to eliminate as they were on the Azerbaijan question. But if you read this book carefully, you'll learn how to eliminate at least one choice on almost any SAT multiple-choice question, if not two or even three choices.

What good is it to eliminate just one or two choices on a four-choice SAT question?

Plenty. In fact, for most students, it's an important key to earning higher scores.

Here's another example:

2

What is the capital of Qatar?

A) Paris

B) Dukhan

C) Tokyo

D) Doha

On this question you'll almost certainly be able to eliminate two of the four choices by using POE. That means you're still not sure of the answer. You know that the capital of Qatar has to be either Doha or Dukhan, but you don't know which.

Should you skip the question and go on? Or should you guess?

Close Your Eyes and Point

There is no guessing penalty on the SAT, so you should bubble something for every question. If you get down to two answers, just pick one of them. There's no harm in doing so.

You're going to hear a lot of mixed opinions about what you should bubble or whether you should bubble at all. Let's clear up a few misconceptions about guessing.

FALSE: Don't answer a question unless you're absolutely sure of the answer.

You will almost certainly have teachers and guidance counselors who tell you this. Don't listen to them! The SAT does not penalize you for wrong answers. Put something down for every question: you might get a freebie.

FALSE: If you have to guess, guess (C).

This is a weird misconception, and obviously there is nothing magical about the letter (C). Since the SAT is a standardized test, there will be no way to game the system by just selecting a certain answer. The test-makers take great pains to have a fairly even answer distribution on each test, and we'll tell you how you *can* benefit from that in a minute.

FALSE: Always pick the [fill in the blank].

Be careful with directives that tell you that this or that type of answer is always right. It's much safer to learn the rules and to have a solid guessing strategy in place.

As far as guessing is concerned, we do have a small piece of advice. First and foremost, make sure of one thing:

Answer every question on the SAT.
There's no penalty.

Letter of the Day (LOTD)

Sometimes you won't be able to eliminate any answers, and sometimes there will be questions that you won't have time to look at. For those, we have a simple solution. Pick a "letter of the day" (from A to D), and choose that answer choice for questions you can't eliminate any answers on or do not have time to do.

This is a quick and easy way to make sure that you've answered every question. (Remember, you are not penalized for wrong answers!) It also has some potential statistical advantages. If all the answers show up about one-fourth of the time and you guess the same answer every time you have to guess, you're likely to get a couple of freebies.

LOTD should absolutely be an afterthought; it's far more important and helpful to your score to eliminate wrong answers before you guess. But for those questions you don't know at all, LOTD is better than full-on random guessing or no strategy at all.

POOD, Pacing, POE, and LOTD all work together to help you spend your time where it does the most good: on the questions you can and should get right.

The Best Way to Bubble In

Work a page at a time, circling your answers right on the test booklet. Transfer a page's worth of answers to the answer document at one time. It's better to stay focused on working questions rather than disrupt your concentration to find where you left off on the answer document. You'll be more accurate at both tasks. Do not wait until the end, however, to transfer all the answers from one section to your answer document. Bubble one page at a time on Writing and Language and on Math, and bubble a passage at a time on Reading. In the last few minutes of each section, though, bubble the answer after working each question.

Be Ruthless

The worst mistake a test-taker can make is to throw good time at "bad" questions. You read a question but don't understand it, so you read it again. And again. If you stare at it really hard, you know you're going to just see the answer. And you can't move on, because really, after spending all that time it would be a waste not to keep at it, right?

Wrong. You can't let one tough question drag you down, and you can't let your worst instincts tempt you into self-defeating behavior. Instead, the best way to improve your SAT score is to follow our advice.

- Use the techniques and strategies in Step 7 to work efficiently and accurately through all your Now and Later questions.

- Know your Never questions, and use your LOTD.

- Know when to move on. Use POE, and guess from what's left.

In Step 7, you'll learn how strategies such as POOD, Pacing, and POE work on each section.

Use Your Pencil

You own the test booklet, and you should write where and when it helps you. Use your pencil to literally cross off wrong answers on the page. On the Reading Test, use your pencil to underline proof for the answer in the passage. On the Writing and Language Test, use your pencil to underline the task you're asked to do. On the Math Test, set up questions with pencil and paper and write down your work. You'll learn more details about how to use your pencil in Step 7.

Step 7: Learn Section-Specific Strategies

SAT Reading

Structure

The SAT Reading Test consists of five passages, each with 10–11 questions. The passages will include one literature passage, two social studies or history passages, and two science passages. One of the passages will be a "dual" passage: it will contain two shorter passages that are related in some way. One of the social studies passages and one of the science passages will include charts or graphs. Each passage on the SAT Reading begins with a blurb that gives the author, title, and date of the passage. The passages are all roughly the same length—about 500–750 words.

Pacing

Once you have determined your goal score for the Reading Test, there are two possible approaches to pacing: choose passages or choose questions. Some people have very high accuracy when they take their time working a passage; these people get their highest scores by starting with the more straightforward passages, spending a bit more time per passage, and using their Letter of the Day on harder passages. Other people maximize their scores by working the question types they are best at from all five passages.

For illustration, imagine that your goal is to work forty-two questions and guess your Letter of the Day on ten questions. If you choose passages, you will work all of the questions from four passages and guess your Letter of the Day on all of the questions from one passage. If you choose questions, you will work forty-two questions selected from all five passages and guess your Letter of the Day on ten questions. You can try both strategies to see which works better for you.

POOD

The passages are not written in order of difficulty, so you must determine your Personal Order of Difficulty. When determining your POOD, consider the passage's genre and topic. For example, if you love to read fiction but your eyes glaze over when you read history, you may want to start with the literature passage and leave a history passage for last.

You should also consider the year the passage was written. A passage written in 1850 is likely to have tougher language than a passage written in 2010.

Choose your Personal Order of Difficulty for the following set of passages based on their blurbs.

This passage is adapted from Gloria Steinem, *My Life on the Road*. ©2015 by Random House.

This passage is adapted from Malcolm Macleod, "Some Salt with Your Statin, Professor?" ©2014 by PLOS Biology.

Passage 1 is adapted from P.G. Hubert, "Occupations for Women." Originally published in 1894. Passage 2 is adapted from Virginia Penny, *Think and Act*. Originally published in 1869.

This passage is adapted from Chuck Gill, "Zombie ant fungi 'know' brains of their hosts." Originally published in 2014 by the Penn State College of Agricultural Sciences.

This passage is adapted from Wendy Koch, "Has the U.S. Really Reached an Epic Turning Point in Energy?" ©2015 by The National Geographic Society.

Write down the titles of the passages in your Personal Order of Difficulty.

1st _____

_____

2nd _____

_____

3rd _____

_____

4th _____

_____

5th _____

_____

There's no right answer—it's whatever makes sense for your POOD.

5-Step Basic Approach

No matter your pacing goals and Personal Order of Difficulty, you will need an efficient approach to the Reading Test.

Your task on the SAT Reading Test is quite different from what you're asked to do in your English class at school. In your English class, you might spend days or even weeks reading a book. You might learn about its author and the time in which it was written. You discuss the book in class, and your teacher might help you uncover its central themes. You might be graded on your thoughtful participation in class discussions. Perhaps you take a test during which you're expected to remember key points about the book. Maybe you write an essay about the book in which you're rewarded for your independent, critical thinking.

On the SAT Reading Test, not so much. On the SAT, you get points for bubbling in the right answer, period. Your task is different, so your approach needs to be different.

You get points for answering questions, not for reading the passage, so you shouldn't spend your time reading the whole passage. On the other hand, the correct answers to the questions are based on the passage, so you need to read the relevant parts of the passage carefully. To balance these goals, you need an approach that helps you focus on the right information in the passage in order to answer the questions. The following 5-step process is designed to do just that.

Read the blurb.

Read the blurb that precedes the passage. Previewing the blurb gives you some context for what you are about to read. Without this step, it's as though you've walked into the library, grabbed a random book, opened to a random page, then started to read. Not a very friendly way to begin!

> This passage is adapted from Eric M. Keen, "Why Are Blue Whales So Gigantic?" ©2020 by Scientific American.

What genre does this passage belong to—literature, science, or social studies?

_____

_____

If you chose "science," you're right.

What is the passage's topic?

_____

_____

The passage is about the size of blue whales.

STEP 2» Select and Understand a Question

Take a look at the set of questions that accompanies the Blue Whales passage. (We've removed the answer choices for now.) Which questions ask about a specific part of the passage, and which ask about the passage as a whole? What do you notice about the order of the specific questions?

43

The primary purpose of the passage is to

44

Which conclusion is best supported by the passage?

45

Which choice provides the best evidence for the answer to the previous question?

46

The author includes the quote in line 1 ("We are...giants") in order to present

47

The passage suggests that rorquals differ from the first baleen whales in that

48

As used in line 30, "modes" most nearly means

49

The author suggests that which of the following is a challenge blue whales face because they feed primarily on krill?

50

Which choice provides the best evidence for the answer to the previous question?

51

According to the figure, right whales share their suborder with which of the following species?

52

According to information in the figure and in the passage, how are the largest and second largest animal species related to one another?

The first three questions are general questions that ask about the passage as a whole, and the last two questions refer to a figure. The rest of the questions are about specific parts of the passage. On SAT Reading, the specific questions appear in an order that roughly matches the progression of the passage. In this set of questions, notice that the line reference for question 46 comes before the line reference for question 48. The questions without line references are also in order. For example, you'll likely find that question 47 asks about a part of the passage that falls between the lines for question 46 and the lines for question 48. If you work the specific questions in order and leave the general questions for last, the answers are easier to find.

So, start with the first specific question you see. In this case, work question 46 first.

You'll notice that the College Board likes to phrase questions as odd, half-finished sentences.

46

The author includes the quote in line 1 ("We are...giants") in order to present

Rephrase these half-sentences as actual questions that begin with words such as "What" or "Why." Be sure you understand the question you should answer.

How would you rephrase question 46?

_____

_____

One possible way to phrase the question is "Why does the author include the quote in line 1?"

Read What You Need

Most SAT Reading questions can be answered based on 10–12 lines in the passage. We call this the "window" for the question. You usually don't need to read more than this, but you also should not read less. Even if the question mentions line 4, you can't get the answer by reading only line 4.

Here is the Blue Whales passage. Remember, you don't need to read the whole passage. Just locate the window for question 46 and draw a bracket around it to remind yourself of how much you need to read. You're looking for about 10–12 lines around line 1.

"We are truly living in a time of giants." Lofty language like this doesn't happen often in scientific literature. But the person who wrote them, biologist Jeremy Goldbogen, understands: When it comes to writing about whales, the scale and mystery of their lives can be difficult to overstate. For the past two decades, Goldbogen and his network of collaborators have been piecing together a puzzle: Whales are the largest animals to have ever lived—but why? The puzzle pieces were out of reach until the turn of the current century, and in only the last few years have there been enough in place to grasp the bigger picture.

We now understand that whale gigantism is tied closely to two things: one, their choice of prey, and two, the coincidence of their evolution with a global increase in the upwelling of nutrient-rich water from the depths of the ocean. The first baleen whales to evolve filter-fed upon plankton—essentially, tiny, drifting sea bugs. But a more recent lineage, known as the rorquals, developed a remarkable new feeding strategy known as "lunge feeding", which allowed them to access a different type of prey: swarming schools of small fish and krill. The mechanics of this strategy align such that bigger mouths (and hence larger bodies) profit more from lunge feeding than smaller mouths or alternative modes of feeding. And so the advent of lunge feeding (about seven to 10 million years ago) provided the energetic incentive structure for enormous size, and a sudden rise in ocean upwelling (approximately five million years ago) provided them with ample prey supply: a serendipitous recipe for bigness.

It may be clear why rorqual whales are so large in general, but of these giants, why are blue whales so much larger than all the others? A blue whale can grow to more than 100 feet long and weigh over 150 tons. Compare this to the fin whale, the second largest animal ever: typically 80 feet long and 60 tons—less than half the blue whale's weight. What's going on here? What makes blue whales so special?

[O]f all present-day rorquals, blue whales are arguably the most specialized. They eat krill and only krill, with very few exceptions. This, as we will see, is the key to their superlative size. To specialize in krill is no small task. Krill can be superabundant, but only within certain isolated regions of the world ocean, such as upwelling zones and polar oceans. To stumble upon booms of krill yet survive the inevitable busts, blue whales need extreme mobility and large energy reserves. They achieve these with enormous size, sleek bodies, and small, hydrodynamic flippers. Such bodies travel more efficiently through water, and thick stores of energy-rich blubber pile on helpful momentum.

But once found, krill are not so easy to catch. A successful lunge has to be executed at speed and with an element of surprise. Some whales can outmaneuver krill, such as the long-flippered humpback whale, but blue whales have had to sacrifice maneuverability for the sake of long-range efficiency. In the arms race against krill escape, the blue whale's best option is a larger mouth, which it achieves with a larger body. Yet again, the solution is size.

Bigness is key to the blue whale's diet, but bigness also adds to the whale's overall energy budget. A bigger body requires more food, which even fewer portions of the world ocean
75 can support, thus requiring a bigger body that can travel even further with larger energy stores and greater efficiency. But a bigger body requires even more krill … and with each turn of the crank, the blue whale's precarious life strategy
80 becomes ever more tenuous.

And this is how the blue whale has become trapped within a tautological circle of specialization: it needs to be big enough in order to eat enough to be big. The means and the
85 end have become one and the same. Ecological entrenchment has become entrapment. The only way to get out, somehow, is to get bigger. This is why the blue whale has become the largest, by far, of the Earth's whales.

Which lines did you bracket as the window for question 46?

Lines 1–14 work well. You'll often find that a paragraph is a good window for a question.

Once you have found the window for the question, read with the question in mind. Why did the author include the quote in line 1? As you read, have your pencil in hand, and underline the parts of the text that answer the question.

We've reprinted the window for question 46 for convenience.

Bookmark this page so you can easily flip back to the passage as you work through the rest of the chapter.

"We are truly living in a time of giants." Lofty language like this doesn't happen often in scientific literature. But the person who wrote them, biologist Jeremy Goldbogen, understands: When it comes to writing about whales, the
5 scale and mystery of their lives can be difficult to overstate. For the past two decades, Goldbogen and his network of collaborators have been piecing together a puzzle: Whales are the largest animals to have ever lived—but why? The puzzle
10 pieces were out of reach until the turn of the current century, and in only the last few years have there been enough in place to grasp the bigger picture.

 ## Predict the Correct Answer

As mentioned above, underline the answer to the question in the passage. Predict the correct answer based on what you read, even if the question is not explicitly answered in the text. Do not rely on your memory or your interpretation of the passage.

If you haven't already done so, underline the lines in the paragraph above that explain why the author included the quote, then check your prediction below.

The following sentences provide an answer to the question and are therefore good ones to underline:

> When it comes to writing about whales, the scale and mystery of their lives can be difficult to overstate.

> For the past two decades, Goldbogen and his network of collaborators have been piecing together a puzzle: Whales are the largest animals to have ever lived—but why?

Notice that these sentences are **not** included in the line reference mentioned in the question! Evidence for the correct answer is often found just before or just after the line reference in the question, so you must read a window around it.

Prediction: The author includes the quote to introduce the topic that scientists are interested in: why are whales so large?

STEP 5 » Use POE

Eliminate answer choices that don't match the prediction from the passage. Be sure to read all four answers, even if you see one that looks good right away. The best answer is the one that is best supported by the passage.

Try eliminating the answers that don't match the prediction above.

46

The author includes the quote in line 1 ("We are…giants") in order to present

A) a fun fact about fairy tale creatures.

B) an observation that has sparked researchers' interest.

C) a complaint from a short person.

D) a warning of the danger of being stepped on.

Did you eliminate (A), (C), and (D)? Nice work!

Of course, the wrong answers are usually not quite so easy to eliminate. In fact, the answer choices can be one of the trickiest elements of the SAT Reading test. Think about it: if the wrong answers were easy to eliminate, or if the correct answer was obvious, then everyone would get just about every question correct. Let's pause question 46 for a minute and talk about the College Board's answer choices.

Getting Underneath the Answer Choices

When the SAT Reading authors create a question, they use specific strategies to make the correct answer less obvious and to make the wrong answers more tempting. On many questions, the correct answer will be a paraphrase of what was in the passage. You'll need to match the paraphrased words of the answer back to the words in the passage.

On the other hand, wrong answers often use exact words from the passage. That makes them look like what you've read, and they can be tempting if you're working too quickly. However, if you pay attention to each word of a wrong answer, you'll see that it doesn't quite match what the passage said. Or, you may see that it matches something stated in the passage, but that it doesn't answer the right question. You might also see an answer choice that sounds logical, but if you try to point to evidence for it in the passage, you'll see that it just isn't there.

Let's take a look at the previous question with some more realistic answer choices.

46

The author includes the quote in line 1 ("We are…giants") in order to present

A) an overstatement of the scale of whales' lives.

B) an observation that has sparked researchers' interest.

C) a type of language uncommon in scientific writing.

D) a phrase first used in literature but adopted by scientists.

What are the test writers up to with these answer choices?

Choice (A) includes several words you saw in the window for the question. However, the answer doesn't match what the passage actually says: according to the passage, it is *difficult to overstate* the scale of whales' lives.

Choice (C) is actually true: the passage says, *Lofty language like this doesn't happen often in scientific literature.* However, (C) doesn't answer the right question—why did the author include the quote? It was used to introduce a topic of interest, **not** to show a type of language uncommon in scientific writing.

Choice (D) could be true: the quote may originally have come from literature. However, on SAT Reading, you must be able to point to proof for the correct answer in the passage. There is no mention of literature in the passage. As far as the College Board is concerned, Jeremy Goldbogen is the genius who coined that phrase.

Now that you know what the College Board is up to, how can you improve your accuracy? Make sure your predictions are based on what is actually stated in the passage. Then, focus on Process of Elimination, crossing out answer choices that aren't supported by the passage.

Repeat Steps 3 through 5

Continue to work through the specific questions in order, repeating steps 3 through 5 for each question.

Let's try the next question.

47

The passage suggests that rorquals differ from the first baleen whales in that

Rephrase the question: How are rorquals different from the first baleen whales? Unlike the previous question, question 47 doesn't include a line reference that tells you where to look for the answer. In that case, how will you find the window for the question?

Some questions include words that appear in the passage—we call these "lead words." You can scan the passage for the lead words to help you find the window. Question 47 includes the lead words *rorquals* and *baleen whales*.

It would take too long to scan the whole passage looking for a single word. Luckily, you don't have to! You noticed earlier that the order of the specific questions matches the progression of the passage. Question 46 asked about line 1 and question 48 asks about line 30. Therefore, the answer to question 47 is probably somewhere between those two lines. You've already read the first paragraph, so start with the second paragraph and scan for the lead words *rorquals* and *baleen whales*.

Did you find them? They appear in lines 20 and 23. Read a window of 10–12 lines, and underline a prediction in the text.

What's your prediction?

_____

_____

The text says, *The first baleen whales to evolve filter-fed upon plankton—essentially, tiny, drifting sea bugs. But a more recent lineage, known as the rorquals, developed a remarkable new feeding strategy known as "lunge feeding," which allowed them to access a different type of prey: swarming schools of small fish and krill. The mechanics of this strategy align such that bigger mouths (and hence larger bodies) profit more from lunge feeding than smaller mouths or alternative modes of feeding.*

There are a few differences between rorquals and the first baleen whales mentioned in these lines, and that's okay: just underline these lines and eliminate answers that don't match the prediction.

A) the first baleen whales evolved a new lunge feeding strategy, whereas rorquals perfected filter-feeding.

B) the first baleen whales were dependent on nutrient-rich water, whereas rorquals evolved after a decrease in ocean upwelling.

C) very large bodies are beneficial to rorquals, whereas the first baleen whales didn't require such extreme size.

D) baleen whales are marine mammals, whereas rorquals are a type of drifting insect.

Choice (A) can be eliminated because it directly contradicts the passage, which says that the *first baleen whales to evolve filter-fed upon plankton* and that *rorquals developed a remarkable new feeding strategy known as "lunge feeding."* Choice (D) also clearly doesn't match the passage, which calls *plankton*, not *rorquals, drifting insects*.

That leaves you with (B) and (C). Getting down to two answer choices is a common occurrence on SAT Reading. On harder questions, the match between the correct answer and the passage might not be obvious at first, so you'll need a good strategy for working with tougher answer choices.

POE: Use Two Passes and Compare

Make two passes through the answer choices. On the first pass, eliminate answers that clearly don't match the prediction. Leave an answer in if you're not sure about it or if it's confusing and requires a more careful read.

On the second pass, take your time. At this point, you're probably choosing between the right answer and a tricky wrong answer that sounds a lot like the right answer. Use a comparison process: compare the remaining answer choices to each other and focus on the differences between them. Then, compare the answer choices to the passage. Consider each word of the answer as you match it back, and eliminate answer choices that don't match the meaning of the passage. Keep in mind that the correct answer may not use exactly the same words that the prediction does. Finally, compare each answer choice to the question that was asked, and eliminate answers that don't answer the right question.

Now, try a comparison strategy with the two remaining answer choices from question 47.

A)

B) the first baleen whales were dependent on nutrient-rich water, whereas rorquals evolved after a decrease in ocean upwelling.

C) very large bodies are beneficial to rorquals, whereas the first baleen whales didn't require such extreme size.

D)

Each answer choice gives a statement about *the first baleen whales* and a statement about *rorquals*. Focus on the statements about one type of whale. Choice (B) says that *rorquals evolved after a decrease in ocean upwelling*, and (C) says that *very large bodies are beneficial to rorquals*. Match each statement back to the passage. Lines 22–36 state, *a more recent lineage, known as the rorquals, developed a remarkable new feeding strategy known as "lunge feeding"... and a sudden rise in ocean upwelling...provided them with ample prey supply: a serendipitous recipe for bigness.* Therefore, it was *a rise in ocean upwelling*, rather than *a decrease in ocean upwelling*, that prompted the rorquals' evolution. Eliminate (B). Lines 26–36 state, *The mechanics of this strategy align such that bigger mouths (and hence larger bodies) profit more from lunge feeding than smaller mouths or alternative modes of feeding.* Since the passage states that rorquals developed the lunge feeding strategy, rorquals must benefit from *very large bodies*. By contrast, the first baleen whales did not use the lunge feeding strategy, so they *didn't require such extreme size*. Choice (C) matches the passage, and it's the correct answer.

Notice that although the correct answer didn't use the exact words from the passage, it was directly supported by evidence that you could underline.

The comparison process will help you choose between tricky answer choices. However, if you get stuck, take a guess, and move on to a question that will give you an easier point.

Now, let's take a look at some of the other types of questions you'll see on SAT Reading.

Vocabulary-in-Context Questions

`48`

As used in line 30, "modes" most nearly means

The question asks what the word *modes* means as it is used in line 30. We call this a "vocabulary-in-context" question, and each passage typically has one or two of them. They usually involve a common word that has multiple definitions. The key to answering a vocab-in-context question correctly is to pay attention to the way the word is used within the passage.

Read a window around the line reference. Typically, you only need to read one or two sentences as the window for a vocabulary-in-context question. The text says, *The mechanics of this strategy align such that bigger mouths (and hence larger bodies) profit more from lunge feeding than smaller mouths or alternative modes of feeding.* Next, cross out the word *modes*, and jot down another word or phrase that has a

similar meaning. Be sure to base your prediction on the text. Here, the word *modes* could be replaced by the word "strategies." Now, eliminate answers that don't match the prediction.

A) trends.

B) moods.

C) statuses.

D) methods.

The words *trends*, *moods*, and *statuses* do not match "strategies," so eliminate (A), (B), and (C). The word *methods* matches "strategies." The correct answer is (D).

You may have noticed that the wrong answers are related to other meanings of "modes." Alternative definitions are very common wrong answers on vocabulary-in-context questions, so be sure to make a prediction based on the way the word is used in the passage rather than on your outside knowledge of the word's meaning.

Paired Evidence Questions

Question 49 is the first question in a paired set. We'll consider its paired evidence question—question 50—in a moment. But first, try question 49. Then check the explanation that follows.

The author suggests that which of the following is a challenge blue whales face because they feed primarily on krill?

A) Blue whales must adapt to contend with an uncertain supply of prey.

B) Blue whales must compete with other rorquals for food.

C) Blue whales have gained maneuverability at the expense of long-range efficiency.

D) Blue whales must travel in small pods in order to surprise their prey.

The question asks for a *challenge* faced by *blue whales* as a result of the fact that they *feed primarily on krill*. Since there is no line reference, use lead words and the order of the questions to find the window. Questions 47 and 48 asked about the second paragraph, and there was no mention of blue whales in the second paragraph. Starting with line 37, scan the passage looking for the lead words *blue whales* and *krill*. The third paragraph mentions blue whales, but krill are not mentioned until line 47.

Read a window around the lead words. The text says that blue whales *eat krill and only krill, with very few exceptions* and that to *specialize in krill is no small task. Krill can be superabundant, but only within certain isolated regions of the world ocean, such as upwelling zones and polar oceans. To stumble upon booms of krill yet survive the inevitable busts, blue whales need extreme mobility and large energy reserves.*

Underline the lines that discuss a *challenge blue whales face because they feed primarily on krill*. Underline *Krill can be superabundant, but only within certain isolated regions of the world ocean, such as upwelling zones and polar oceans. To stumble upon booms of krill yet survive the inevitable busts, blue whales need extreme mobility and large energy reserves.*

Eliminate answers that don't match this prediction.

Choice (A) matches the prediction: the phrase *inevitable busts* indicates that there are times when blue whales don't find enough krill, which supports *an uncertain supply of prey*, and *blue whales need extreme mobility and large energy reserves* indicates that the whales have had to *adapt* by developing these qualities. Keep (A).

Choice (B) doesn't match the prediction. Although it could be true that blue whales *compete with other rorquals*, the passage doesn't mention that as a challenge. Eliminate (B).

Choice (C) doesn't match the prediction, and it mixes up words from the passage. In the next paragraph, the text says, *blue whales have had to sacrifice maneuverability for the sake of long-range efficiency*. Choice (C) gets it backwards, saying that whales sacrificed *long-range efficiency* for *maneuverability*. Eliminate (C).

Choice (D) doesn't match the prediction; the passage doesn't say that blue whales must *travel in small pods*. Eliminate (D).

The correct answer is (A).

Now let's look at question 50.

50

Which choice provides the best evidence for the answer to the previous question?

Question 50 is a paired evidence question. Since it asks for the lines that provide evidence for the previous question, all you need to do is look at the lines you underlined when you were making your prediction for question 49. The prediction came from lines 50–56. Eliminate answers that don't include these lines.

A) Lines 22–26 ("But a…krill")
B) Lines 53–56 ("To stumble…reserves")
C) Lines 62–63 ("A successful…surprise")
D) Lines 63–67 ("Some…efficiency")

Only (B) includes any of the lines from the prediction, so it's the correct answer.

A paired evidence question can be a buy-one, get-one-free gift. When a best evidence question is paired with a specific question that is easy to find, work the first question on its own. Then, to answer the best evidence question, simply choose the lines you underlined when you made your prediction for the previous question. Buy one, get one free!

However, sometimes best evidence questions are paired with general questions, or with questions that are hard to locate in the passage. Questions 44 and 45 (which you skipped at first) are an example of a general paired evidence set. Those questions are best left for after the specific questions, so we'll come back to them.

Charts and Graphs Questions

Two of the passages on the SAT Reading (one social sciences passage and one science passage) will include charts or graphs. When you work a question about a chart or graph, read the figure carefully: read the title, the variables that are measured, the units, and the key (if provided). Eliminate answers that don't match the information in the chart or graph. Some charts and graphs questions also ask about the passage. If a question asks about both the figure and the passage, read the relevant part of the passage carefully and eliminate answers that don't match the passage.

Here is the figure that accompanies the Blue Whales passage.

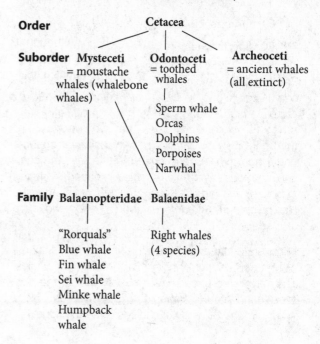

Marine Mammal Species Grouped by Order, Suborder, and Family

Let's try the first question about the figure.

51

According to the figure, right whales share their suborder with which of the following species?

A) Mysteceti

B) Sei whale

C) Odontoceti

D) Sperm whale

Carefully read the chart. According to the title, the chart shows *Marine Mammal Species Grouped by Order, Suborder, and Family*. The first tier gives the *order*, the second tier gives the *suborder*, and the third tier gives the *family*. The word *species* appears under *right whales*, and since the title says the chart shows *marine mammal species grouped by order, suborder, and family*, it's reasonable to think that the lists given under *Odontoceti* and *Balaenopteridae* are also species.

Next, understand the question: which species shares a suborder with right whales? First locate right whales. They are listed under *Balaenidae*. Next find the *suborder* connected to *Balaenidae*. It is *Mysteceti*. Now, work through the answer choices using the figure.

Choice (A) is *Mysteceti*. Be careful! Right whales belong to the suborder Mysteceti, but the question asks for another *species* that shares the same suborder. Choice (A) answers the wrong question, so eliminate (A).

Choice (B) is *Sei whale*. The *sei whale* is listed under the family *Balaenopteridae*, which is connected to the suborder *Mysteceti*. Therefore, right whales share their suborder with sei whales. Keep (B).

Choice (C) is *Odontoceti*. According to the chart, Odontoceti is a suborder, not a species. It is also not connected to right whales, so eliminate (C).

Choice (D) is *Sperm whale*. The *sperm whale* is listed under the suborder Odontoceti, which is not connected to right whales, so eliminate (D).

The correct answer is (B).

Try the next charts and graphs question, then check the explanation below.

52

According to information in the figure and in the passage, how are the largest and second largest animal species related to one another?

A) The largest and second largest animal species belong to different orders.

B) The largest and second largest animal species belong to the same order, but to different suborders.

C) The largest and second largest animal species belong to the same suborder, but to different families.

D) The largest and second largest animal species belong to the same suborder and the same family.

The question refers to both the figure and the passage. It asks *how the largest and second largest animal species are related to one another*. The figure doesn't mention size, so start by scanning the passage for the lead words *largest* and *second largest*. They appear in the third paragraph. Lines 39–44 say, *A blue whale can grow to more than 100 feet long and weigh over 150 tons. Compare this to the fin whale, the second largest animal ever: typically 80 feet long and 60 tons—less than half the blue whale's weight.* The *fin whale* is the *second largest animal*, and since it is smaller than the *blue whale*, the *blue whale* must be the largest animal.

Next, look for the *blue whale* and *fin whale* on the figure. They are listed together under the family *Balaenopteridae*. Now, use Process of Elimination on the answer choices.

Choice (A) doesn't match the figure. All of the species listed in the chart are grouped under the same *order* (*Cetacea*). Eliminate (A).

Choice (B) doesn't match the figure. The family that the blue and fin whales belong to is connected to just one *suborder* (*Mysteceti*), so they must share the same suborder. Eliminate (B).

Choice (C) doesn't match the figure. As noted above, the blue and fin whales are listed together under the family *Balaenopteridae*, so they share the same *family*. Eliminate (C).

Choice (D) matches the information in the figure. The correct answer is (D).

General Questions

Now that you've worked the specific questions, you're ready to come back to the general questions.

General Paired Evidence Questions

As we mentioned before, questions 44 and 45 are an example of a general paired evidence set.

When a best evidence question is paired with a general question (or with a question that is hard to locate in the passage) you can use the answers to the best evidence question to help you work the previous question. We call this "Parallel Process of Elimination." Let's try Parallel POE on questions 44 and 45.

44

Which conclusion is best supported by recent discoveries about whales as described in the passage?

A) The lunge feeding strategy could not have developed without a rise in ocean upwelling.

B) Blue whales evolved about five million years ago.

C) Blue whales' size both helps and hinders their efforts to feed themselves.

D) On average, the blue whale is twice the length of the fin whale.

45

Which choice provides the best evidence for the answer to the previous question?

A) Lines 10–14 ("The puzzle…picture")

B) Lines 41–44 ("Compare…weight")

C) Lines 50–53 ("Krill…oceans")

D) Lines 71–73 ("Bigness…budget")

Question 44 doesn't give you any hints about where to look in the passage—the answer could come from anywhere! Instead of searching the whole passage looking for the answer to question 44 and hoping the evidence appears in question 45, start with the evidence in question 45.

Think for a moment about how paired questions operate. The correct answer to the first question must be supported by an answer to the evidence question, and the correct answer to the evidence question must support an answer to the first question. In other words, if there is an evidence answer choice that doesn't match with an answer choice for the first question, it is wrong. Period. Likewise, if there is an answer choice for the first question that isn't supported by an evidence answer choice, it too is wrong. Period.

Use this to your advantage. Consider the lines for each answer choice in the evidence question. For each choice, ask yourself, "Do these lines answer the previous question? Do they support any of the answers to the previous question?" If an evidence answer choice answers the right question and supports a first question answer choice, draw a line connecting the matching answer choices. If not, eliminate the evidence answer choice. When you're through, any answer choice in the first question that isn't connected to an evidence answer choice must also be eliminated.

44. Which conclusion is best supported by recent discoveries about whales as described in the passage?

A) The lunge feeding strategy could not have developed without a rise in ocean upwelling.

B) Blue whales evolved about five million years ago.

C) Blue whales' size both helps and hinders their efforts to feed themselves.

D) On average, the blue whale is twice the length of the fin whale.

45. Which choice provides the best evidence for the answer to the previous question?

A) Lines 10–14 ("The puzzle...picture")

B) Lines 41–44 ("Compare...weight")

C) Lines 50–53 ("Krill...oceans")

D) Lines 71–73 ("Bigness...budget")

First, read the lines for (45A). These lines state, *The puzzle pieces were out of reach until the turn of the current century, and in only the last few years have there been enough in place to grasp the bigger picture.* These lines don't give a *conclusion* supported by recent discoveries; they say only that we have recently begun to understand the puzzle. Therefore, these lines do not address question 44. Furthermore, these lines don't match any of the answer choices for question 44. The lines for (45A) can't possibly provide the best evidence for question 44. Eliminate (45A).

The lines for (45B) indicate that the *fin whale* is *typically 80 feet long and 60 tons—less than half the blue whale's weight.* These lines don't support any of the answer choices for question 44. Note that (44D) compares the lengths of the fin and blue whales instead of their weights. Eliminate (45B).

The lines for (45C) state, *Krill can be superabundant, but only within certain isolated regions of the world ocean, such as upwelling zones and polar oceans.* These lines do not support any of the answer choices for question 44, so eliminate (45C).

The lines for (45D) state, *Bigness is key to the blue whale's diet, but bigness also adds to the whale's overall energy budget.* These lines support (44C), so draw a line connecting (44C) with (45D).

Since there is no support for (44A), (44B), and (44D) in the answer choices for question 45, eliminate them. The correct answers are (44C) and (45D).

General Questions

In addition to general paired evidence questions, general questions include main idea, primary purpose, and general structure questions. It's best to leave general questions for last because working the specific questions helps you get to know the passage.

At this point, you're well prepared to work a general question about the Blue Whales passage. Use what you've learned from the specific questions to work question 43. Then, check the explanation below.

43

The primary purpose of the passage is to

A) compare the feeding strategies of various whales.

B) highlight characteristics common among large species.

C) outline key points in the evolution of marine mammals.

D) provide an evolutionary explanation for an unusual trait.

The question asks for the *primary purpose* of the passage. In the first paragraph, the author poses a question: *Whales are the largest animals to have ever lived—but why?* In the following paragraphs, the author explains why whales—especially blue whales—evolved to be so large. Eliminate answers that don't match this prediction.

Eliminate (A) because the passage as a whole does not focus on comparing feeding strategies. Instead, feeding strategy is one of the components in the explanation of whales' unusual size.

Eliminate (B) because the passage does not focus on *characteristics common among large species*. Instead, the passage focuses on explaining the size of one large species (the blue whale).

Eliminate (C) because it is too broad—the passage focuses on the evolution of the blue whale, not *the evolution of marine mammals* in general.

Choice (D) matches the prediction—the *unusual trait* is extreme size. The correct answer is (D).

Dual Passage

One passage in the Reading Test will be a dual passage, that is, two shorter passages on a common topic. The passages will be followed by some questions that are only about one passage or the other and some questions that ask you about both passages. Thinking about one passage at a time is easier than thinking about two at once, so the best strategy is as follows:

---

1. Work the questions about Passage 1 using the 5-Step Basic Approach.

2. Work the questions about Passage 2 using the 5-Step Basic Approach.

3. Jot down the main idea of each passage.

4. Work the questions that ask about both passages.

When you work the questions about both passages, it may help to use Process of Elimination based on one passage at a time. Remember, if you run out of time, or if you find the questions about both passages especially tough, you can use your Letter of the Day.

Here is a short excerpt from a dual passage. Let's try a few questions that ask about both passages. Remember that, in an actual dual passage set, you would first work the questions that ask about Passage 1 and then the questions that ask about Passage 2, becoming familiar with both passages in the process. For now, simply read the excerpt from each passage, then jot down the main idea of each excerpt.

Passage 1 is adapted from John Dewey, *Democracy and Education*. Originally published in 1916. Passage 2 is adapted from W.E.B. Du Bois, Editorial. Published in *The Crisis* July 1915. ©1915 by the National Association for the Advancement of Colored People.

Passage 1

…The primary ineluctable facts of the birth and death of each one of the constituent members in a social group determine the
Line necessity of education. Even in a savage tribe, the
5 achievements of adults are far beyond what the immature members would be capable of if left to themselves. With the growth of civilization, the gap between the original capacities of the immature and the standards and customs of the
10 elders increases. Mere physical growing up, mere mastery of the bare necessities of subsistence will not suffice to reproduce the life of the group. Deliberate effort and the taking of thoughtful pains are required. Beings who are born not only
15 unaware of, but quite indifferent to, the aims and habits of the social group have to be rendered cognizant of them and actively interested. Education, and education alone, spans the gap.

What is the main idea of Passage 1?

_____

_____

Passage 2

...But wait; is work the object of life or is life the object of work? Are men to earn a living or simply to live for the sake of working? Manifestly
Line
55 life, and abundant life, is the object of industry and we teach men to earn a living in order that their industry may administer to their own lives and the lives of their fellows. If, therefore, any human being has large ability it is not only for his advantage but for the advantage of all
60 society that he be put to the work that he can do best. While we teach men to earn a living, that teaching is incidental and subordinate to the larger training of intelligence in human beings and to the largest development of self-realization
65 in men.

What is the main idea of Passage 2?

_____

_____

One way to express the main idea of Passage 1 is that education is necessary to maintain the customs of a social group.

One way to express the main idea of Passage 2 is that education is about more than earning a living; education helps people develop their full potential.

Now try the questions about both passages.

39

In developing their respective arguments, the authors of Passage 1 and Passage 2 both highlight the

A) gap between elders and the immature.

B) importance of education for society.

C) opposing needs of the individual and the group.

D) necessity of earning a living.

The question asks what the authors of both passages highlight. Eliminate answers that misrepresent either passage.

Start by thinking about Passage 1.

Choices (A) and (B) seem okay based on Passage 1, so keep (A) and (B) for now.

Eliminate (C) because, although Passage 1 discusses what is necessary for the group, it doesn't mention *opposing needs of the individual*.

Eliminate (D) because Passage 1 does not discuss *earning a living*.

Now use Process of Elimination based on Passage 2. Eliminate (A) because Passage 2 doesn't discuss *elders and the immature*. Keep (B) because it matches both passages. The correct answer is (B).

40

Which choice best represents the views presented in Passage 1 and Passage 2, respectively?

A) Passage 1 regards education as a challenge that must be carefully planned for, whereas Passage 2 considers teaching and learning to be natural human inclinations.

B) Passage 1 presents learning as essential, whereas Passage 2 describes intellectual training as a privilege enjoyed by those who have secured the basic necessities for survival.

C) Passage 1 claims that the abilities of individuals are meant to serve the group, whereas Passage 2 argues that earning a living is secondary to developing intellect.

D) Passage 1 focuses on the necessity of education in order to preserve society, whereas Passage 2 considers the importance of education for realizing individual potential.

The question asks which choice best represents the views presented in Passage 1 and Passage 2. Use Process of Elimination, considering one passage at a time. Based on Passage 1, eliminate (C)—Passage 1 doesn't discuss *the abilities of individuals*. Now consider Passage 2. Eliminate (A) because Passage 2 doesn't state that teaching and learning are *natural human inclinations*. Eliminate (B) because Passage 2 doesn't state that training is a *privilege enjoyed by those who have secured the basic necessities for survival*. Keep (D) because it matches both passages. The correct answer is (D).

41

It can most reasonably be inferred from Passage 2 that Du Bois would describe "the mere mastery of the bare necessities of subsistence" (lines 10-11, Passage 1) as

A) essential.

B) challenging.

C) inadequate.

D) inspiring.

The question asks how Du Bois would describe *the mere mastery of the bare necessities of subsistence*, which is a quote from Passage 1. First, use the line reference to find the window from Passage 1. The text says, *Mere physical growing up, mere mastery of the bare necessities of subsistence will not suffice to reproduce the life of the group.* Therefore, the *mere mastery of the bare necessities of subsistence* means learning only what's needed for physical survival.

Next, look for the point of view expressed in Passage 2. The last sentence of Passage 2 says, *While we teach men to earn a living, that teaching is incidental and subordinate to the larger training of intelligence in human beings and to the largest development of self-realization in men.* In other words, the author of Passage 2 thinks that people should learn more (*the larger training of intelligence* and *the largest development of self-realization*) than only what they need to survive (*earn a living*). Therefore, his view is that the *mere mastery of the bare necessities of subsistence* is not enough. Eliminate answers that don't match this prediction.

Essential, *challenging*, and *inspiring* do not match the prediction "not enough." Eliminate (A), (B), and (D). Choice (C), *inadequate*, matches "not enough." The correct answer is (C).

42

Which choice from Passage 2 provides the best evidence for the answer to the previous question?

A) Lines 51–52 ("But wait . . . work")

B) Lines 52–53 ("Are men . . . working")

C) Lines 57–61 ("If . . . best")

D) Lines 61–65 ("While . . . men")

The question is the best evidence question in a paired set. Since you were able to answer question 41 on its own, simply look at the lines used to answer question 41. The prediction for question 41 was based on the last sentence of Passage 2. The correct answer is (D).

That's a Wrap

As you have seen, everything you need to answer the questions on the SAT Reading Test is located in the passage. Focus on finding the evidence and eliminating the answers that don't match it, and you will improve your SAT Reading score!

Summary

- Decide which pacing approach works best for you: choose passages or choose questions.

- Use your Personal Order of Difficulty to choose the easier passages and work them first.

- Follow the 5-Step Basic Approach:

  1. Read the Blurb

  2. Select and Understand a Question—translate the question stems into actual questions

  3. Read What You Need—read 10–12 lines of context

  4. Predict the Correct Answer—underline a prediction in the text

  5. Use POE—eliminate answers that don't match the prediction

- If there is more than one answer left, use comparison:

  - ❏ Compare the answers to each other

  - ❏ Compare the answers to the question

  - ❏ Compare the answers to the passage

- Dual Passage

  - ❏ Work the questions about Passage 1

  - ❏ Work the questions about Passage 2

  - ❏ Jot down the main idea of both passages

  - ❏ Work the questions about both passages, thinking about one passage at a time

SAT Writing and Language

Structure

The Writing and Language section comes second on the SAT, after Reading. It consists of 44 questions spread out over 4 passages. The questions cover a variety of topics related to punctuation, grammar, and style, but they are not organized by topic or difficulty level. Remember that the Writing and Language Test and the Reading Test make up your verbal score equally. This section is very rule-based, so it can be easier to improve than the Reading section simply by learning the rules.

Pacing

You'll have 35 minutes to answer the 44 questions. Some people don't have much trouble getting through all 44 questions in this amount of time, but others find themselves rushing through the last passage. Of course, this means those students who rush will likely miss questions toward the end of the test that they could have gotten right, simply because they ran out of time. If you find that you fall into this group, it will be in your best interest to have a plan that involves skipping some questions as you go, especially if you don't have time to learn the rules that are tested on the Writing and Language portion. How should you decide which questions to skip?

POOD

Earlier, we discussed POOD (Personal Order of Difficulty)—throughout the SAT, you should start with the questions and passages that are easiest for you in order to maximize your score. How does this work on the Writing and Language Test? Well, the Writing and Language Test does not follow an order of difficulty: there won't be harder or easier passages, and the easy and hard questions are all mixed together. Furthermore, you don't have much time per question, so you may waste time if you try to skip around. Lastly, you will need to answer questions that involve the structure and flow of ideas within a passage; this means that you should be reading the paragraphs within a passage in order.

With all of this in mind, it's in your best interest to complete the Writing and Language section more or less in order. However, that does not mean that you have to *attempt* every question. You may find that skipping a few of the hardest Writing and Language questions gives you more time to finish the test and get to those questions at the very end that you may not otherwise have had time to do—some of which are likely easy. The good news is that it is easy to identify many of the hardest and most time-consuming questions on the Writing and Language: they are much longer.

Take a look at these two questions:

1

A) NO CHANGE

B) famous and well-known

C) famously well-known

D) well-known

9

The writer is considering deleting the phrase "since Tolstoy's death in 1910" and ending the sentence with a period after the word "changed." Should the phrase be kept or deleted?

A) Kept, because it contributes to the essay's biographical sketch of the author of *War and Peace*.

B) Kept, because it introduces a topic of discussion that is continued throughout the paragraph.

C) Deleted, because the remainder of the paragraph describes the insignificance of Tolstoy's death.

D) Deleted, because the paragraph as a whole is focused on the achievements of another author.

Which question looks easier? #1! This question has no more than three words in each answer, and you can probably eliminate (B) and (C) without even reading the sentence. To answer this question, all you'll need to do is read the sentence in the passage and see which option makes the most grammatical sense. On the other hand, question 9 requires you to read the preceding sentence *and the entire rest of the paragraph*, consider whether the phrase is consistent with the paragraph, and then read four long answer choices and use POE. Whew! Is one point worth all of that work? For many people, the answer will be no.

Here is the key pacing strategy for the Writing and Language Test:

Make the obvious POOD choice and finish the Writing and Language Test.

Skip the obviously more time-consuming questions as you go so that you will be able to make it to the end of the section in 35 minutes and not have to rush on easier questions at the end. Remember, bubble in the Letter of the Day for any questions you skip. Note that you can circle any questions you skip so that you can attempt them if you have extra time left at the end.

The Basic Approach

The Writing and Language Test is organized into four passages. You don't want to start by reading an entire passage—remember, you don't have a lot of time in this section. Instead, while you are reading each passage, you'll answer the questions as you come to them. Therefore, the first step for Writing and Language is to...

STEP 1 » Read to the end of the sentence with an underlined portion.

Most Writing and Language questions won't actually ask a question—they'll look like question 1 on the previous page. Rather than looking for errors and considering every possible rule related to punctuation, grammar, and style, take a peek at the answers: the similarities and differences among them will tell you what is being tested. For instance, if the words all stay the same but commas change, you know the question is testing you on commas, so you only need to remember comma rules and don't have to worry about any of the other topics to answer that question. Here's step two:

STEP 2 » Look to the answers to see what's changing.

Once you know what topic or topics are being tested, use the rules to determine which answer is correct. Here's the catch: you don't want to try to fix the sentence in your head. You might decide, for example, that a period should be used instead of a comma. However, when you look at the answers, you don't see an answer that has a period. Or worse yet, you may see an answer that does use a period but makes an error with grammar. To avoid picking a trap answer and to save time, therefore…

Use Process of Elimination.  STEP 3

Physically cross off any answer choices that you know are wrong, until you find the one answer that is correct.

Let's take a look at how to apply these steps.

It sounds like the ideal job to many: video game tester. These <u>**1** employees are trying out games</u> features and having a blast.

1

A) NO CHANGE
B) employees' are trying out games'
C) employees are trying out games'
D) employees are trying out game's

Once you have read the entire sentence, look at the answer choices and determine what's changing: apostrophes. The original has no apostrophes, but some of the answer choices have an apostrophe in the first word or in the last word. Let's start with *employees*. You may remember from school that an apostrophe on a noun shows possession. Are the employees owning anything? No, so eliminate (B) because it has an apostrophe on *employees*. Now, look at *games*. Does something belong to the games? Yes, the *features* do. Therefore, there should be an apostrophe on *games*. Eliminate (A). Last, consider where the apostrophe should go. Choice (D) puts the apostrophe on *game*, singular. Is the sentence talking about just one game? No, it means the features of multiple games, so eliminate (D). Therefore, (C) is the answer.

Notice that in the question above, you could easily have made a mistake if you just noticed one of the potential errors. For instance, if you saw right away that *games* should be changed to *games'*, you could have accidentally picked (B) without realizing that (B) creates a new error by adding an incorrect apostrophe to *employees*. This is why it's so important to look for what's changing in the answers and to use POE with the answers that are actually there. Remember, if you try to correct the sentence in your head, you may find that your correction doesn't actually appear in the answers. You're better off using POE!

In the previous question, you needed to know some rules about apostrophes. What other rules do you need to know for the Writing and Language? Let's take a look.

The Big Three

You don't need to learn every rule of English writing to do well on the SAT Writing and Language: you only need to know the handful of rules that are actually tested on the SAT. Moreover, if you decided to study grammar, you would learn terms such as *independent clause*, *parallelism*, *past participle*, *subjunctive mood*, and *possessive determiners*. Just reading those words might start to make your head spin, but remember—no matter what the rules are called, the fancy-sounding names for those rules are NOT tested on the SAT. You should know what the rules are, but you don't need to have a special name for each one. Instead, we'll focus on three key words: Consistent, Precise, and Concise. Let's take a closer look at each one and how it is tested on the SAT.

Consistency

The underlined portion must always be consistent with the non-underlined portion. This is why you must read the whole sentence, and sometimes more than that. Many different grammar topics fall under consistency. Let's take a look at a few of them.

Unfortunately, the job is not as much fun as it sounds: a worker testing video games 2 doesn't just get to sit down and play through the game.

2

A) NO CHANGE

B) don't

C) didn't

D) haven't been able to

First, look to see what's changing in the answer choices: verbs. Many students find it easiest to start with tense. Look for clues in the non-underlined portion that let you know what tense the underlined verb should be in. This sentence has the present tense verb *is* and there is no shift in time, so the underlined verb should also be in present tense. Eliminate (C) and (D) because they aren't in present tense.

Next compare (A) and (B). *Doesn't* is singular—you can test this by putting it with the singular pronoun "it": the correct phrase is "it doesn't." *Don't* is plural, and it goes along with the plural pronoun "they," as in "they don't." A verb must be consistent with its subject. Here, the SAT is trying to trick you. The writers of the test want you to think the subject is *video games*, making the subject and verb combination "video

> Don't be afraid to pick NO CHANGE! It's correct about one-fourth of the time that it appears.

games don't," which probably sounds okay. However, are the *video games* sitting down? No, it is the *worker* doing something in this sentence. The subject of the sentence is *worker*, and the phrase *testing video games* is just a describing phrase that separates the subject and the verb. Now that you know the subject is *worker*, what do you think about the phrase "a worker...don't?" You probably think it isn't correct, and you're right! The word *worker* is singular, so the underlined verb must be singular in order to be consistent. You can cross off (B) because it is plural, so the correct answer is (A). By the way, (D) is also plural, so that's another reason to cross it off.

Video game testers conduct QA, or quality assurance, before a game is released to make sure that [3] they do not have any bugs, glitches, or mistakes.

3

A) NO CHANGE

B) he or she does

C) it does

D) one does

What's changing in the answers? Pronouns. You may remember from school that pronouns stand in for nouns. This means they must be consistent with the nouns they are supposed to be replacing. Start by identifying what person or thing needs to *not have*

any bugs: it's *a game*. Because *game* is singular, the correct pronoun must also be singular. Eliminate (A) because *they* is plural. Again, you can notice how the SAT writers are trying to trick you: *they* could refer back to the *testers*, but the *testers* aren't the ones who could have *bugs, glitches, or mistakes*. Check the remaining options. The pronouns *he* and *she* are not used to refer to video games, so eliminate (B). While *one* is singular, it does not clearly refer back to *a game* in this sentence. The pronoun *it* is the correct pronoun to refer back to *a game*, so the answer is (C). Again, it's all about consistency!

The [4] interesting tasks entry-level testers are assigned could include turning a game on and off hundreds of times to see how long it takes to load, playing one level repeatedly to work out any bugs, or even playing for a whole day and night to ensure that the game can operate for such lengthy spans.

4

The writer wants to emphasize that testing video games is not always exciting. Which choice most effectively accomplishes this goal?

A) NO CHANGE

B) technological

C) necessary

D) tedious

First off, do you notice what's different about this one? It actually asks a question! Although the majority of the questions will look like the ones we've seen before, with no question at all, some Writing and

Language questions will actually ask you something. **The most important thing you can do is notice when you're being asked a question**—otherwise, if you go straight to the answer choices, you can easily pick an answer that you personally like but that does not do what the question is asking you to do. Look at what you are being asked to do here: choose an answer that will *emphasize that testing video games is not always exciting*. Choice (A) does the opposite by describing the tasks as *interesting*. Choices (B) and (C) might sound good in the sentence or might be accurate ways to describe the tasks, but they don't do what the question is asking! They don't relate to the idea that the tasks are *not always exciting*. Choice (D) does fulfill this purpose: *tedious* means "boring" or "repetitive," so it's consistent with the purpose stated in the question. For these questions, the wrong answers will be grammatically correct, but they just don't do what the question is asking. It's a good habit to underline what these questions are asking, and then cross off any answers that are not consistent with that purpose.

You will also see questions that involve the order of ideas, main points of paragraphs and passages, and adding or deleting text. These, too, all come down to consistency. Be sure to pay attention to what you are reading about, as you will need to understand the main idea of the paragraph for many of the ones that ask a question.

Precision

The second of our key words is Precise. SAT correct answers must be precise: that is, they should provide a clear meaning. It's not the reader's job to interpret what the author might have meant; it's the author's job to present the ideas in a clear and precise way. Since you are editing the passage, you'll be tasked with making the text clear and precise. Let's see how this can be tested.

In addition to being patient and methodical, game testers need some knowledge about how games work, and they need to have strong communication skills in order to ⑤ conserve problems to programmers in clear and detailed manner.

---

⑤

A) NO CHANGE

B) convey

C) reply

D) release

Here, vocabulary is changing in the answer choices. Don't worry—in most cases, you will know the words that appear in the answers on the Writing and Language Test. However, you will need to determine which one provides the most precise meaning within the sentence. The sentence states that testers need *strong communication skills in order to* do something, so this blank should have something to do with communication. The word should mean something similar to "communicate." Choice (A), *conserve*, means "not use too much," which doesn't match with "communicate." Choice (B), *convey*, does mean "communicate," so keep this one, but still check (C) and (D). *Reply* means "say back," which doesn't quite match with "communicate," and it isn't correct to say "reply problems." *Release* means "let go of," which doesn't match with "communicate." Therefore, (B) is the answer. As you can see, for these questions it's a good strategy to determine what the underlined portion should be like before you use POE in the answers. This way you know what you are looking for. The correct answer needs to make the meaning of the sentence precise.

Although the job can be monotonous at times, it's extremely important within the video game industry: customers won't be happy if [6] it has bugs, especially those that affect gameplay, and a company can accordingly lose significant amounts of money.

6

A) NO CHANGE

B) a game

C) one

D) that

First, check what's changing in the answers: pronouns but also an actual noun (*a game* in (B)). Consider the difference between a pronoun like *it* and a noun like *a game*. Is the sentence precise? Is it clear what the pronoun *it* refers back to? No—the word *it* could refer to *the job* or *the video game industry* or something else entirely. Since the underlined word is something that could have *bugs*, presumably the word refers to a video game. This isn't clearly indicated by the word *it*—nor would the pronouns *one* or *that* solve the problem—so (B) is the correct answer. Only (B) provides a precise meaning by clarifying what might have bugs. Remember, it's not the reader's

> Note that (B) is a little longer than the other options, but it's more precise. Precise comes before Concise for a reason—don't assume a shorter answer is automatically correct.

job to interpret what a text means. You must pick an answer that makes the meaning 100% clear.

Concision

Some of the SAT Writing and Language questions on the Writing and Language section of the SAT will ask you to choose the option that is concise and doesn't repeat the same words twice or use more words than it needs to. Whew, that was a mouthful! We probably could have said that in a more concise way. You saw in some of the previous questions that the shortest option isn't always correct, but once you have dealt with Consistent and Precise, you can then consider which option is the most Concise. Let's take a look.

A company that makes video games must consider all of the possible ways players might interact with the game and test each one [7] at least one or possibly more times.

7

A) NO CHANGE

B) repeatedly, over and over.

C) more than once and possibly many times.

D) multiple times.

Begin by asking what's changing in the answers. In this case, the wording changes. You might notice something odd with the original underlined portion: it's a bit repetitive. *At least one* already implies that this testing could happen more than once, so (A) is incorrect because the phrase *or possibly more* is redundant. Choice (B) is similar: *repeatedly* means the same thing as *over and over*, so there is no need to use both of those phrases. Choice (C) is not as obviously redundant, but compare it with (D): do the extra words in (C) contribute to the meaning of the sentence? No, (C) and (D) offer the same meaning, and (D) is shorter, so it's the correct answer.

Remember, do not automatically choose the shortest option. Ask yourself whether the extra words make the meaning more precise. If they do, then you want the additional words. In this case, the extra words do not make the meaning clearer.

Visual issues **8** that relate to what players see on the screen can be relatively simple to fix, but errors that affect the way the game is programmed can be time-consuming and challenging to repair.

8

A) NO CHANGE

B) that players can view on-screen

C) related to what is seen

D) DELETE the underlined portion.

First, determine what's changing in the answers: wording. You probably noticed something different here as well. Choice (D) gives the option to delete the phrase entirely. Consider whether the underlined portion is needed or whether it could be deleted. The sentence already describes the issues as *visual*, so it's unnecessary to say that they are related to *what players see*, and (B) and (C) say the same thing with different words. The phrase isn't needed at all, so the answer is (D).

When you have the option to DELETE, look for a reason not to choose it. If the underlined portion is necessary to make the sentence complete, consistent, or precise, then don't choose DELETE. However, if the underlined portion isn't necessary within the sentence, then go with that option.

Punctuation

A final topic that appears on the SAT Writing and Language is punctuation. You looked at apostrophes at the beginning of this lesson. The other types of punctuation you can expect to see tested are commas, periods, semicolons, colons, and dashes. You probably know some rules related to these from school, such as that only a complete sentence can end with a period. So what does a complete sentence need?

Subject + Verb

A complete sentence needs a subject and a verb. Here are two examples:

The reporter writes

My cat is sleeping

Both of these could stand alone as complete sentences, so we call them complete ideas. Some sentences need more than just a subject and a verb. Consider the following:

The reporter has

My cat likes

Even though these phrases contain both a subject and a verb, some verbs, like *has* and *likes*, require an object. The sentence feels like it's missing something—and it is. To make a complete sentence, you need to finish the idea by telling what the reporter has or what the cat likes.

Longer phrases can also be incomplete:

Because I like being outside in warm weather

This idea is incomplete because it starts with *because*. Phrases beginning with *because*, *though*, *when*, *that*, and *since*, among other transition words, are incomplete and must be linked to a complete idea.

Let's take a look at how punctuation and complete sentences could be tested on the SAT.

Game testers must write detailed reports about any errors they find and exactly what they were **9** doing; because programmers need to be able to replicate the glitches in order to find and fix their causes.

9

A) NO CHANGE

B) doing because

C) doing. Because

D) doing: because

First, check what's changing in the answers—in this case punctuation. Next, determine whether the parts of the sentence are complete or incomplete ideas. The part before the punctuation, *Game testers must write detailed reports about any errors they find and exactly what they were doing*, could be its own sentence, so it is a complete idea. The phrase *because programmers need to be able to replicate the glitches in order to find and fix their causes* couldn't be its own sentence—it's incomplete. One answer you should be able to cross off right away is (C): as we discussed, a period can only come after a complete sentence. The second half here isn't complete, so it can't be its own sentence. Now, let's introduce a new rule: a semicolon works just like a period, so (A) is also wrong. Let's compare (B) and (D). Is there any reason to use a colon before *because*? No! You probably already knew that no punctuation is typically used before a phrase beginning with *because*. Therefore, (B) is the answer.

Although this quality assurance testing isn't always as fun as it sounds, the job has its **10** rewards; testers can earn decent wages, and they get to try the newest games long before they are released.

10

A) NO CHANGE

B) rewards. Testers,

C) rewards; testers,

D) rewards, testers

What's changing in the answers? Punctuation. Start by evaluating the parts of the sentence before and after the punctuation: *Although this quality assurance testing isn't always as fun as it sounds, the job has its rewards* is a complete idea, and *testers can earn decent wages, and they get to try the newest games long before they are released* is also a complete idea. Your first thought might be to use a period, since each of these ideas could be its own sentence, but

remember that a semicolon works just like a period. Therefore, hold on to (A), (B), and (C). What about (D)? You may remember from school that a comma in between two complete ideas creates a run-on sentence, so (D) is wrong. Now, the remaining options all work to connect two complete ideas, so what is the difference? Choices (B) and (C) have a comma after *testers*. Is there a reason to use a comma after that word? No, there isn't a reason for a comma there, so eliminate (B) and (C). The correct answer, therefore, is (A).

If you haven't mastered the different types of punctuation, check out our book *Princeton Review SAT Prep* for more on how each punctuation mark can be used.

That's All, Folks!

As you can see, you don't need to be a grammar expert to do well on the SAT Writing and Language. By focusing on the a few key terms and some basic rules, you can boost your Writing and Language score.

Summary

- Aim to finish the Writing and Language section, even if that means skipping a few obviously time-consuming questions as you go.

- Follow the Basic Approach for Writing and Language:

    1. Read to the end of the sentence with an underlined portion.

    2. Look to the answers to see what's changing.

    3. Use Process of Elimination.

- Use the three key words:

    ☐ **Consistent**—make the underlined portion match up with the non-underlined portion.

    ☐ **Precise**—choose an answer that makes the meaning 100% clear.

    ☐ **Concise**—after applying consistency and precision, then choose the option that provides the correct meaning with the fewest words.

- Learn the rules of punctuation to avoid having to guess on those questions.

SAT Math

Structure

The Math portion of the SAT can be found in the third and fourth sections of the test. The third section is a 25-minute, no-calculator section with 15 multiple-choice questions and 5 grid-in questions. The fourth section, which is the final required scored section, is a 55-minute, calculator-permitted section with 30 multiple-choice questions and 8 grid-in questions. The multiple-choice questions have 4 answers, and the grid-ins are free-response questions. Some questions will be grouped together based on the same information, but most are stand-alone questions. Within the multiple-choice section and then starting over within the grid-in section, the questions are arranged in order of difficulty, with many questions rated as "medium" difficulty by College Board. The two Math sections are used to calculate a Math score on a scale of 200–800.

Pacing

Each section of the Math Test gives you less than a minute and a half, on average, to answer each question. Of course, some questions will take less time than that, but others will take more. Unless you are an SAT Math superstar, you are unlikely to be able to work through and answer all 58 questions within the time limit. In fact, we tell most of our students that they should be skipping some questions. Say you rush through the Math Test, trying every question and making a lot of careless mistakes. Perhaps you would end up getting only 30 of the 58 questions right, which would give you a Math score of about 530. What if, instead of trying to tackle everything, you slowed down and only worked the 40 questions that you felt most comfortable with? You'd likely get most or all of them right, and you would never even have to think

about those harder questions. If you were able to get 35 of those 40 correct, your score would jump to a 560 or 570, and you'd get there with a lot less stress! But how do you know which questions to do and which to skip?

POOD

Although the questions in the Math sections are roughly in an order of difficulty, knowing that is not very helpful to you as a test-taker. It is much more useful for you to determine your Personal Order of Difficulty (POOD). College Board rates a question as "easy," "medium," or "hard" based on the number of students that get the question wrong. This does not mean that the concept is inherently difficult, though. Those "hard" questions may just be trickier (more on that later). When you take the Math Test, don't let yourself get stuck on a question that is hard for you. The worst thing you can do is spend a long time on a hard (for you) question when there are still easy (for you) questions left to be done. The way to avoid this is to use a two-pass system.

The Two-Pass System

Do the Math Test in two passes. On your first pass through the section, your job is to decide whether each question is one you want to do Now, Later, or Never. You do the easy questions in the first pass because they're easy, and you don't want to miss any of the easy points. All questions have the same value, so you don't get bonus points for struggling successfully to answer a really tough question. Therefore, you want to make sure you get to all the Now questions that you know how to do. Because they don't put all the questions that you know how to do in one place, the only way to find them is to use this two-pass system.

On the first pass, you also "do" the Never questions because they're not worth the time they would take. Let's say you can't do trig graphing, and on your first pass you come to a trig graphing question. Spending any time on this question would be a waste, so you don't want to come back to it later. You also don't want to leave it blank on your answer sheet, because you might get lucky and guess correctly (remember that there's no penalty for wrong answers). So, put in your Letter of the Day (LOTD) and move on, looking for more questions you know how to do.

That leaves the Later questions. On the first pass, as you identify questions you think you can do but that will take some work, circle them in your test booklet but don't work them. You don't want to get hung up on them before you are sure you've answered all the easy questions, but you want to be able to easily find them again. Once you've worked your way through the entire section in this way (finishing your first pass), you're going to come back and work on the questions you circled and skipped.

> Reminder: Your Letter of the Day (LOTD) is a single letter (A, B, C, or D) that you choose whenever you're purely guessing on a question.

On the second pass, go back and work on the questions you circled in the first pass, starting with the ones in which you are most confident. Spending time on questions you think you may be able to figure out is much wiser than taking a ten-minute nap at the end of the section. When you have five minutes left, stop and make sure to enter your answers for questions you've worked but not marked on your bubble sheet yet. Also put in your LOTD for any questions you're not going to have time to finish.

Using your LOTD along with proper pacing is a very powerful strategy. In our previous pacing example, getting 35 of the 58 questions correct would give you a Math Test score of 560 or 570. If you got there by only doing 40 questions, you would use your LOTD on the remaining 18 questions. The odds are that you'd get about one-fourth of them right, gaining you about 4 more points. This could boost your score up to a 600 with no additional work!

Content

Knowing which topics will come up on the test and focusing first and foremost on the ones you know you can nail will help you to improve your score. The Math sections of the SAT put a heavy emphasis on algebra and algebraic manipulation. You will be expected to create, interpret, and manipulate equations in a variety of formats. You will also need to know how to identify the graphs of functions and find intercepts. A significant portion of questions will require you to interpret and analyze data from charts, graphs, and tables. Finally, a few questions about geometry, trigonometry, and complex numbers will appear as well.

So now you know the topics you'll see on the SAT on test day. What you *don't* know is which questions will be the hard ones and which will be the easy ones. Use this topic list and the results of your first practice test to determine what you need to be studying. Because there's no calculus, don't bother with studying calc. Because there are only a handful of trig questions, you probably don't want to spend too much time on trig either. If you didn't do so well on analyzing data, you need to spend more time doing practice in that area. Finally, if there is any algebra content on the SAT that you haven't studied for a while, you are going to need to review those topics in order to do well on the test.

Remember Your Calculator

You are only allowed to use a calculator on the fourth section of the SAT. Sometimes it will be useful for those questions, and sometimes it won't. They say that every question on the test can be done without a calculator, and they're right. However, doing the test this way is no fun at all, so remember to bring your calculator.

> If you don't have your calculator handy right now, you should. You'll need it to do some of the Math questions in this book. Remember: always have your calculator when doing SAT Math questions that allow for calculator use.

Keep in mind that not all calculators are permitted on the SAT. You can check the College Board's website (www.collegeboard.org) for the specifics. Basically, if your calculator can access the Internet, has a QWERTY keypad, uses an electrical outlet, or is just the calculator app on your phone, you can't use it on the SAT. Don't think that you'll be able to sneak a banned calculator by the proctors, either. College Board has been pushing its proctors to crack down, and they are checking more carefully than they used to.

Even though you *can* use your calculator on all the Math questions in section 4, that doesn't mean that you *should* always use it. Let's look at an example of a question on which you may be tempted to use your calculator, but doing so may be more trouble than it is worth.

$$g(x) = \frac{2}{3}x + c$$

In the function above, c is a constant. If $g(9) = 3$, what is the value of $g(-6)$?

A) -7

B) -3

C) 2

D) 3

In this kind of question, all of the pieces are given to you. All you need to do is the math—carefully. The SAT likes to use negatives, so keep your eyes open for those. Set up the problem on paper before you begin stabbing at your calculator: College Board knows exactly the types of mistakes that can occur when you rush to punch numbers into your calculator too quickly and will have those incorrect solutions waiting for you in the answer choices. In function notation, the value in the parentheses is the value for x that goes in to the function and $g(x)$ is the value that comes out of the function. You should

> Notice that this question has the image of a calculator beside it. This means that this question is from a calculator-permitted section. Any questions in this book with a calculator symbol are from the calculator section of the SAT. Of course, just because you can use your calculator on a given question doesn't mean that you should. Writing out the steps on paper is often the best way to go. If you don't see a calculator symbol, solving with paper and pencil is the only way to go!

recopy the equation with 9 in place of x and 3 for $g(x)$, like so:

$$3 = \frac{2}{3}(9) + c$$

To find the value of $\frac{2}{3}(9)$ using a calculator, you might type it in as $(2 \times 9) \div 3$ or $(2 \div 3) \times 9$, or even $2 \times (9 \div 3)$. All those calculations will give you the same result, but it can get confusing. Doing the math on paper, the 9 is divisible by 3, so you can just cancel those out, which leaves the following:

$$3 = 2(3) + c$$

This simplifies to $3 = 6 + c$, then subtract 6 from both sides to get $c = -3$. Notice that this is the answer in (B). However, the question doesn't ask for the value of c, so that answer is likely a trap. Now the function can be written as follows:

$$g(x) = \frac{2}{3}x - 3$$

Plug in $x = -6$ to get $g(-6) = \frac{2}{3}(-6) - 3$. Simplify the right side using the same steps you used before, on paper or on the calculator, to get $g(-6) = -4 - 3$ or $g(-6) = -7$.

The correct answer is (A), and writing the steps out on paper is a more foolproof way to solve it than using a bunch of parentheses on your calculator. Now let's look at another way to avoid a lot of calculations.

The Big Technique: Ballparking

As you already know, every Math question on the SAT has one right answer and three wrong answers. Your job is to eliminate those wrong answers and pick the right one, rather than just hoping the right one jumps out at you. When the people who write the SAT are constructing a Math question, the first answer they come up with is the right answer. Then, they build the wrong answers by working the problem and making the sorts of mistakes that a careless (or rushing) student might make. The wrong answers they get are what they use as the wrong answers on the test. That's why when you screw up on a question, you frequently find your wrong answer listed. Sneaky, eh?

In order to reduce the chance of this happening, and in order to help you get rid of some wrong answers on questions you're not exactly sure how to do (which will help you guess better), you're going to use a technique called Ballparking.

Ballparking is the name for the process of reading a question, figuring out roughly what the right answer will be (without actually working the problem), and then crossing out any answers that are too big, too small, or too obviously trying to trick you.

For example, if a question says that the price of something increases 20 percent from $300, you can immediately cross out anything less than $300 because the price is going up, not down. You could also get rid of anything bigger than $600 because it goes up only 20 percent, which is much less than doubling. It's likely that $320 would be an answer choice on this question because that's what you get when you add $20 instead of 20%. They're trying to trick you, so turn the tables and cross off that answer.

Ballparking will rarely eliminate all three wrong answers, but it will frequently eliminate one or two wrong answers, and that's a real help. Try it out on these problems. (Don't work them out—just practice eliminating answers that are too large or too small for right now.)

5

If 12 cans of food can feed 8 dogs for one week, how many cans of food would be needed to feed 6 dogs for two weeks?

A)   9

B)   12

C)   16

D)   18

A Note on Question Numbering
You may notice that the practice questions found in this book, particularly in the Math chapters, are not always numbered sequentially. In other words, you may see Math questions numbered 6, 7, 13, 32, and 37, for example. We've done this to indicate where a given question may show up on the actual exam and thus help you anticipate where a certain topic may be tested and how.

13

	Candidate A	Candidate B	Candidate C	Total
Virginia	7,713	9,244	3,377	20,334
Maryland	4,320	4,253	1,025	9,598
Delaware	1,760	1,963	487	4,210
Pennsylvania	4,410	5,686	2,392	12,488
Total	18,203	21,146	7,281	46,630

Based on the survey data, for which state is the ratio of votes for Candidate B to votes for Candidate C closest to the ratio of the total votes for Candidate B to total votes for Candidate C for all of the survey participants in the four states?

A) Virginia

B) Maryland

C) Delaware

D) Pennsylvania

In question 5, try to estimate before you calculate. If 12 cans will feed 8 dogs for one week, then 12 cans can feed 4 dogs for 2 weeks. Since you need to feed 6 dogs for 2 weeks, the answer must be greater than 12. Eliminate (A) and (B). Once you get rid of those answers, you have a better chance of guessing the correct one (it happens to be (D)) or avoiding traps if you make a mistake calculating the answer.

In question 13, you could use your calculator to find the exact ratio of the total of those who voted for Candidate B to those who voted for Candidate C and that same ratio for each of the states. The numbers on the chart are not pretty, though, so this could take up precious time. Instead, round the values and estimate the ratios first. For the totals, the numbers are about 21,000 to 7,000 (roughly) for an estimated ratio of 3 to 1 or just 3.

Now round and calculate the ratios for each state as follows:

A) Virginia   9,000:3,000   estimated ratio of 3

     Keep (A).

B) Maryland   4,000:1,000   estimated ratio of 4

     Eliminate (B).

C) Delaware   2,000:500   estimated ratio of 4

     Eliminate (C).

D) Pennsylvania 6,000:2,000   estimated ratio of 3

     Keep (D).

That leaves you with (A) and (D), so you now have a fifty-fifty chance of getting this right. To determine the exact answer, you would need a calculator to find that the ratio in Virginia is closer to 3, so the correct answer is (A).

Since we just dealt with a word problem, let's talk about a consistent approach to use when faced with these wordy and sometimes difficult questions.

The Big Technique: Word Problem Approach

Use the following steps every time you are faced with a word problem.

STEP 1 » Know the question.

Read the final question before calculating anything, and underline the actual question at the end.

STEP 2 » Let the answers help.

Look for clues on how to solve and ways to use Process of Elimination.

STEP 3 » Break the problem into bite-sized pieces.

When you actually read the question, look for the key information and work with one piece at a time. Watch out for tricky phrasing, and eliminate answers after working each piece.

The Big Technique: RTFQ

When solving long word problems, knowing the question at the end is the first step. But even on questions that look like straightforward, plug-and-chug algebra questions, it is very important to start by Reading the Final Question (RTFQ). As we said before, the "hard" questions are often just trickier, not necessarily more complicated. Let's look at an example.

7

If $\dfrac{4x-1}{3x} = \dfrac{2}{3}$, what is the value of $4x$?

A) $\dfrac{1}{2}$

B) 1

C) 2

D) 3

Read the Final Question to see what you are solving for: it's the value of 4x. You can bet a million dollars that the value of x is one of the trap answers. To avoid picking this, underline *what is the value of 4x* in the question to give yourself a mental and visual reminder of what the answers represent. Now get to solving. Cross-multiply to get $3(4x - 1) = 2(3x)$, which simplifies to $12x - 3 = 6x$. You can now solve for x by adding 3 to both sides to get $12x = 6x + 3$, then subtracting $6x$ to get $6x = 3$, and dividing by 6 to get $x = \frac{1}{2}$. Oh look, that's (A), but you know not to pick it! You won't forget that the question asked for $4x$, not x, so the answer is $4x = 4\left(\frac{1}{2}\right) = 2$, (C).

Now let's look at two more techniques that can help you break down tricky questions, even difficult ones, and make them much more manageable.

The Big Technique: Plugging In

Here is the sort of algebra question that SAT loves to test.

15

The expression $\dfrac{3x-5}{x+2}$ is equivalent to which of the following?

A) $3 - \dfrac{5}{2}$

B) $3x - \dfrac{5}{x+2}$

C) $3 - \dfrac{5}{x+2}$

D) $3 - \dfrac{11}{x+2}$

If you came across this question while taking the SAT, you might think to yourself, "Gaah! I don't want to do this—there are way too many x's here." Well, we agree with you, so we're going to teach you a way to eliminate all of the variables from this question and turn it into a simple arithmetic problem. We'll do it by using one of our most powerful techniques—Plugging In.

The thing about question 15 that makes it troublesome is the variable, right? If the question were asking you to find equivalent numerical fractions, it would be a snap, wouldn't it? So, what you're going to do is make up a value for x and change all the fractions we're comparing into real numbers. Use 2 for x and work the problem out.

If $x = 2$, then the given expression becomes $\frac{3(2)-5}{2+2} = \frac{6-5}{4} = \frac{1}{4}$. Now the question is asking you to find the answer that is equal to $\frac{1}{4}$. This is what we call the target value; circle it.

Now go to the answer choices, plug in 2 for every x (because you picked 2 for x at the beginning, you have to use it all the way through—don't change your value for x in the middle of a question), and see which answer choice works out to $\frac{1}{4}$. That's easy enough.

A) $3 - \frac{5}{2}$ $\frac{6}{2} - \frac{5}{2} = \frac{1}{2}$

That's not $\frac{1}{4}$, so cross it out.

B) $3x - \frac{5}{x+2}$ $3(2) - \frac{5}{2+2} = 6 - \frac{5}{4} = \frac{24}{4} - \frac{5}{4} = \frac{19}{4}$

Eliminate it.

C) $3 - \frac{5}{x+2}$ $3 - \frac{5}{2+2} = 3 - \frac{5}{4} = \frac{12}{4} - \frac{5}{4} = \frac{7}{4}$

Nope, must be (D).

D) $3 - \frac{11}{x+2}$ $3 - \frac{11}{2+2} = 3 - \frac{11}{4} = \frac{12}{4} - \frac{11}{4} = \frac{1}{4}$

That's it!

Choice (D) is the correct answer.

So maybe you're thinking that you got lucky here. Nope, not at all. Plugging In will work on almost any question with variables in the answer choices. As long as you follow the simple steps, you'll get the right answer on Plugging In questions on the test.

Here's how to do it:

Plugging in Basic Approach

STEP 1 ≫ **Assign numbers to all the variables.**

Pick a number for one of the variables, following any requirements in the question. Then see what else you can figure out. If no other values can be determined, assign a number to the remaining variable(s). Clearly label the value you've chosen for each variable.

STEP 2 ≫ **Solve the question using your numbers.**

Circle whatever value you get that answers the question. This is the target value, and you're going to check the answer choices to see which one matches your target value.

STEP 3 ≫ **Put the number that you used for each variable into the answer choices and solve them.**

Eliminate any that do not match your target value from step 2.

STEP 4 ≫ **Check all four answer choices.**

Always check every answer choice. If you get more than one that matches your target value, just use a different set of numbers and try again (this doesn't happen very often, but we'll demonstrate how to handle it later in this chapter anyway).

That's all there is to it.

Pick Easy Numbers

Remember that you still have to do some math when you're plugging in, so pick numbers that are going to make your life easier. We picked 2 in the previous question, not 137.92. It would have worked if we had picked 137.92 (go ahead and try it out if you don't believe us), but why make life so hard? By picking 2, we kept the math simple and barely worked up a sweat finding the right answer.

Keeping that in mind, then, take a look at this:

> Some good numbers to plug in are 2, 4, 5, or 10. Make sure to follow the restrictions in the question when picking your numbers. It is usually best to avoid plugging in 0 or 1, as they make weird things happen with the math.

8

If $\dfrac{c-2d}{c} = \dfrac{5}{9}$, which of the following must also be true ?

A) $\dfrac{c+d}{c} = \dfrac{13}{9}$

B) $\dfrac{d}{c} = \dfrac{2}{9}$

C) $\dfrac{d-2c}{d} = -\dfrac{9}{5}$

D) $\dfrac{d-2c}{d} = \dfrac{9}{5}$

This is a different sort of question—you are no longer solving for one variable in terms of the others. Instead, you need to find a true statement based on an equation. There are variables in the answer choices, though, so plugging in can still help. It is unlikely that you can pick values for c and d simultaneously that will make this equation true. Instead, start with the one that's easy to pick a value for. That means starting with c here, since the denominator is c on the left side and 9 on the right side. If you make $c = 9$, this means that $9 - 2d = 5$, so $2d = 4$ and $d = 2$.

The question asks for a true statement, so there is no target value here. You do have values that work for the given equation, though, so they will make the correct answer true. Just carefully plug $c = 9$ and $d = 2$ into the answer choices to avoid making a mistake.

A) $\dfrac{c+d}{c} = \dfrac{13}{9}$ $\dfrac{9+2}{9} = \dfrac{13}{9}$ $\dfrac{11}{9} = \dfrac{13}{9}$

Nope, not true.

B) $\dfrac{d}{c} = \dfrac{2}{9}$ $\dfrac{2}{9} = \dfrac{2}{9}$

Looks good, but check (C) and (D) too.

C) $\dfrac{d-2c}{d} = -\dfrac{9}{5}$ $\dfrac{2-2(9)}{2} = -\dfrac{9}{5}$

$\dfrac{-16}{2} = -\dfrac{9}{5}$ Again, nope.

D) $\dfrac{d-2c}{d} = \dfrac{9}{5}$ $\dfrac{2-2(9)}{2} = \dfrac{9}{5}$

$\dfrac{-16}{2} = \dfrac{9}{5}$ That's not true, either.

Choice (B) is our answer. So when do you want to plug in? Every single time you can. Just look for variables in the answer choices. It's a foolproof way of getting the questions right, and that's what it's all about on the SAT, right? Right.

Word Problem Plugging In

Plugging In is a hugely powerful technique (on many SAT tests, we've counted more than ten questions that you could do with Plugging In), and you should use it at every available opportunity. This means don't use it just on algebra questions—it is great for word problems too.

21

A house painter estimates that it will take him x hours to paint a house. He promises the homeowner that the actual time will be within 8 hours of that estimate. If the painter keeps his promise and it takes him t hours to paint the whole house, which of the following inequalities accurately expresses the relationship between t and x ?

A) $|t - x| < 8$

B) $x + t < 8$

C) $x > t - 8$

D) $x < |t - 8|$

Say that the painter estimates that it will take 20 hours to complete the job, so $x = 20$. In this case, t could be 27 hours and the estimate would be true. You can put these values into the answer choices and eliminate anything that is not true based on these numbers.

A) $|t - x| < 8$ $|27 - 20| < 8$

This simplifies to 7 < 8.
This is true, so keep it.

B) $x + t < 8$ $20 + 27 < 8$

This simplifies to 47 < 8.
This is NOT true, so eliminate it.

C) $x > t - 8$ $20 > 27 - 8$

This simplifies to 20 > 19.
This is true, so keep it.

D) $x < |t - 8|$ $20 < |27 - 8|$

This simplifies to 20 < 19.
This is NOT true, so eliminate it.

So, two answers worked—what should you do? Cry? Give up? No! You can either guess and go from here, or you can finish this one out by trying something different. Instead of using numbers that make his promise true, use numbers that make the promise *false*. The correct answer should NOT work with numbers that don't meet the painter's promise. Try plugging $x = 20$ and $t = 10$ into the remaining choices.

A) $|t - x| < 8$ $|10 - 20| < 8$

This simplifies to 10 < 8.
Now this is *not* true. Keep it!

~~B) $x + t < 8$~~

C) $x > t - 8$ $20 > 10 - 8$

This simplifies to 20 > 2.
This is true, but you want false.

~~D) $x < |t - 8|$~~

The correct answer is (A). Once you've plugged in the first time, you know the steps to take to check the answers, so plugging in again is easy if you need to do it.

Plugging In also works on geometry questions the same way that it works on other questions. You plug in your numbers, solve for the answer, and then check the answer choices. Remember not to violate any of the rules of geometry, though—no triangles with 300 degrees or squares with five sides!

> Whenever you have variables in the answers, plug in!

The Big Technique: PITA

No, it's not snack time. PITA stands for Plugging In the Answers, another type of Plugging In strategy that you can use on the SAT.

PITA is a technique you can use when the question tells you a little story and then asks you how many or how much. All the answers are real numbers, and only one of them works in the story College Board told (of course—otherwise there'd be more than one right answer). So, what you're going to do on this type of question is try the answers out in the little story. Plug the Answers Into the story. (Okay, so that way it spells PAIT, but you get the idea.)

Plugging In the Answers Basic Approach

 STEP 1 Underline what the question asks for and label the answers accordingly.

If the question asks how many movie tickets were sold to adults, write "*adult tickets*" above the answers. If it asks for the value of *x*, write "*x*" above the top answer. Any time the final question asks for a specific value or number, that quantity is what the answers represent, and you can use PITA to answer the question.

Start with one of the middle answer choices. STEP 2

Unless the question asks for the *least* value or the *greatest* value, start with (B) or (C) and use that number to work through the story. If it is too big or too small, you can eliminate other answers as well.

When you find an answer that works, STOP!  STEP 3

Unlike with Plugging In, there is only one answer that can possibly work on PITA questions. Once you find it, even if it is just because you've eliminated the other three answers, stop and bubble that answer in.

Here's how it works on a real question:

9

Mark goes to the store to buy a new computer. The computer is on sale for 40% off the original price. He then uses a coupon for an additional 15% off the sale price. If the total price (pre-tax) that he pays for the computer is $561, what was the original price of the computer?

A) $1,100

B) $1,020

C) $860

D) $730

You might be tempted to write your own equation, but because it's a multiple-choice question with real values, you don't need to! You can make use of the answers: plug these values into the question and check the result. This eliminates the need to write an equation and helps reduce errors. Here's how Plugging In the Answers works:

The answers are arranged in descending order. Instead of starting with (A), start with one of the middle answers. That way, if it's too low or too high, you can eliminate more than one answer with the first set of calculations.

Always label the answer choices before you start solving the problem, and work horizontally so you can easily see what to do on later answer choices. Let's try it on this one.

Label the answers as "original price" and start with (B). There is a 40% discount, so put that next. If the original price of the computer was $1,020, then with a 40% discount the new price would be 60% of the original price: $1,020(0.6) = $612. Enter this under the "40% discount" heading. Next comes the 15% coupon. With the coupon, the final price would be 85% of the previous price, or $612(0.85) = $520.20. Write this under "15% coupon."

You should write it like this:

	Original price	40% discount	15% coupon	$561?
A)	$1,100			
Start: B)	$1,020	$612	$520.20	TOO SMALL!
C)	$860			
D)	$730			

The computer was supposed to cost $561; there-fore, the result with (B) is not high enough. Only one answer is larger, so the answer must be (A). You can check it out if you like. When plugging in the answers, though, you do not need to try all four as you do with Plugging In. PITA questions always have numbers in the answers, and you only need to check all four answers when using Plugging In because the answers contain variables, and more than one expression with variables could happen to equal the same number.

Original price	40% discount	15% coupon	$561?
A) $1,100	$660	$561	Yep!
Start: B) $1,020	$612	$520.20	NO WAY!
C) $860			
D) $730			

That word problem wasn't too bad, and the story was not that complex. Let's try PITA on one with a more convoluted story.

28

An art teacher has x students in her art class. She has a total budget of y dollars to spend on art supplies for the class. If she spends $4 on supplies per student, then she will be $3 under budget. However, if she spends $5 per student, then she will be $18 over budget. How many students are in the art class?

A) 15

B) 18

C) 21

D) 30

See how there are two different stories here? PITA can help you make sense of them one at a time. Label the answers as "students" and start with (B), 18. Use the first story to figure out the teacher's budget. It should look like this:

	Students	$4 per student	Budget
A)	15		
B)	18	$72	$75
C)	21		
D)	30		

Because the teacher was $3 under budget in the first story, she had a total budget of $72 + $3 = $75. Now use this to see if it works for the second story.

	Students	$4 per student	Budget	$5 per student	Over budget
A)	15				
B)	18	$72	$75	$90	$15
C)	21				
D)	30				

Because she needs $90 to spend $5 per student, this is $90 − $75 = $15 over budget. The questions says that she should be $18 over budget, so cross off (B). There must be more students in the class to push her further over budget, so cross off (A) as well and try (C). It should look like this:

	Students	$4 per student	Budget	$5 per student	Over budget
~~A)~~	~~15~~				
~~B)~~	~~18~~	$72	$75	$90	$15
C)	21	$84	$87	$105	$18
D)	30				

That works! The correct answer is (C). If you weren't sure after (B) whether you needed a bigger or smaller number—never fear! You have the steps all laid out, so even if you ended up having to check (A) and (C), it would *still* be faster and more accurate than writing and solving a system of equations.

Speaking of solving equations, PITA also works very well on questions that may have tricky algebra, such as those that ask you to determine the value of a variable in an equation or inequality.

6

Which of the following values is a solution to
the inequality $\frac{1}{5}(7x-3)<x$?

A) 1

B) 2

C) 3

D) 4

Algebra can get messy sometimes, especially when dealing with fractions and inequalities. To use PITA on a question like this, try out the values in the inequality given. Label the answers as "x," start with (B), and move on from there as needed.

		x				
	A)	1				
Start:	B)	2	$\frac{1}{5}(7(2)-3)<2$	$\frac{1}{5}(14-3)<2$	$\frac{1}{5}(11)<2$	$\frac{11}{5}<2$	Nope
	C)	3				
	D)	4				

Choice (B) didn't work, but it was very close. It may not always be clear which direction to go in next, so just pick a direction and go. Try (A) next.

		x				
	A)	1	$\frac{1}{5}(7(1)-3)<1$	$\frac{1}{5}(7-3)<1$	$\frac{1}{5}(4)<1$	$\frac{4}{5}<1$	True!
Start:	~~B)~~	~~2~~	$\frac{1}{5}(7(2)-3)<2$	$\frac{1}{5}(14-3)<2$	$\frac{1}{5}(11)<2$	$\frac{11}{5}<2$	Nope
	C)	3				
	D)	4				

You're On Your Way!

These simple Math techniques will do a lot to improve your score. If you want more great techniques or a more thorough review of Math content, check out The Princeton Review's *SAT Prep* book.

Summary

- Use the two-pass system to work through the Math section efficiently.

- Use your Personal Order of Difficulty to find all the Now questions and work them first.

- Mark questions that you want to work on Later, and use your LOTD for any Never questions.

- Use your calculator wisely. Make sure to set up the question first and only calculate if you need to do so to avoid making mental math mistakes.

- Use Ballparking to eliminate any answers that are too big or too small. This will help you avoid falling for trap answers and improve your odds if you need to guess.

- For Word Problems, follow this approach:

  1. Know the question—read the entire question and underline the actual question at the end.

  2. Let the answers help—look for clues about how to solve it or for ways to use POE.

  3. Use bite-sized pieces—read carefully and do one small step at a time.

- For every Math question, make sure to Read the Final Question (RTFQ) to avoid solving for the wrong thing or falling for a trap answer.

- For questions with variables in the answer choices, Plug In following these steps:

  1. Pick numbers for all the variables, making sure to follow any requirements given, and write them down.

  2. Solve the question using the numbers you picked to get a target value that answers the question. Circle the target value.

  3. Plug your numbers into the answer choices to eliminate any choices that don't work.

  4. Check all 4 answer choices. If more than one works, plug in again.

- For questions that ask for a specific value, Plug In the Answers following these steps:

  1. Underline the final question and label the answers.

  2. Start with one of the middle numbers unless asked for the *least* or *greatest* value. Use that value to work through the steps of the question and eliminate answers.

  3. When you find an answer that works, STOP!

STEP 8: Next Steps

Congratulations! You've now developed a list of target schools, determined your goal score, and learned the most efficient and effective ways to reach that goal. You have a plan for how to spend your study time, but you'll likely need some resources beyond what we've included in this book. Let's take a look at what is available to you.

Resources from the College Board

The College Board offers a number of printable official SAT tests on its website, or you can purchase a book of them. You can also find some College Board-approved SAT prep materials online. While these resources do come directly from the College Board, remember—that's the company that makes the test. It's not really in the College Board's interest to provide you with tricks to help you score higher. Advice from the test-writers will give you some kind of strategy, but for the most part it will simply reinforce what you have learned in school, which may not be enough to improve your score significantly.

Princeton Review Books

You've started to learn our strategies in this book, and there's good news: we teach the same strategies across all of our SAT books. If you're looking for help on all sections of the test, *SAT Premium Prep* is for you. It includes the basic strategies we discussed in this book as well as more detailed strategies for just about every question type on the test, and it also includes plenty of drills and practice sections. If you are focusing on just one or two sections of the test,

check out *Math Workout for the SAT* or *Reading and Writing Workout for the SAT*. If you have mastered the strategies and are looking for even more practice questions, *10 Practice Tests* will have you covered. It includes ten full-length practice SATs with explanations that use our proven strategies. You can find these titles wherever books are sold, or at your local or school library.

Courses and Tutoring

Some students find they benefit more from an instructor-led course or tutoring session than from taking charge of prep by themselves. If it's in your budget (or offered by your school!), a prep course or tutor can help keep you on track by meeting at a set time and assigning specific homework. Working actively with an expert instructor, even for only a short amount of time, can help you learn and improve more quickly. The Princeton Review offers a variety of online and in-person courses as well as one-on-one tutoring, and by reading this book you already have a good foundation for the strategies we teach in class. You can find more information at www.PrincetonReview.com or by calling us at 1-800-2REVIEW (1-800-273-8439). You can also ask your school guidance counselor about SAT prep that may be offered by your school or in your community.

If you're not sure what prep option is best for you, the following flow chart may help you decide.

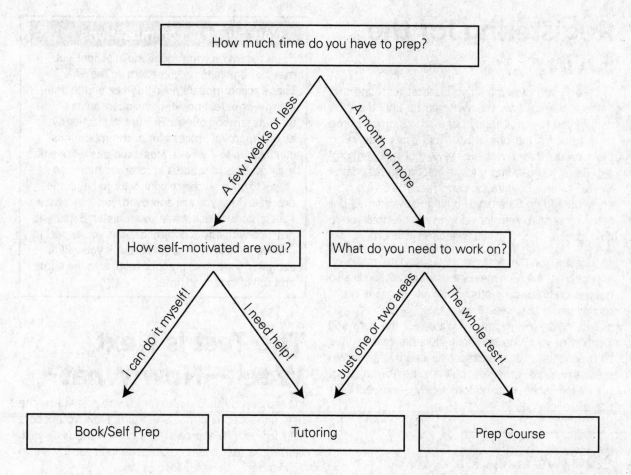

Registering for the SAT

In Step 5, you determined your target test date and made a plan for how you will prep up until that test date. If you haven't already done so, it's a good time to register for the official SAT. This can be done on the College Board website, www.collegeboard.org/sat. There you can find a list of upcoming test dates as well as their registration deadlines. The SAT is generally offered on Saturday mornings seven times per year. It's best to register early to ensure that you're able to take the SAT at your preferred location.

To register for the test, you will need to make an account on the College Board website. You'll also need a credit card or other form of payment and a recent photo that shows your face, for security purposes. When you register, you'll select the date and location of your choice. Most students test at their high schools or at other schools nearby. If you are ready to apply to colleges, you'll also be able to select up to four schools to automatically send your SAT scores to for free.

> Your school may also offer a free school-day SAT. Ask your guidance counselor for more information.

A Note about Accommodations

If you receive accommodations in school, you may be eligible to receive them on the SAT. These accommodations include extended time, a large-print test booklet, and alternate test formats, among others. Be sure to start early, as the approval process for accommodations can take up to 7 weeks. Most students work with their schools to request accommodations, so speak to your guidance counselor to begin the process. Once you are approved, you'll receive a special code to use when you register. Be sure to practice with any accommodations you expect to receive on test day—for example, if you will have extended time, take practice tests with the same amount of extended time.

The Test is Next Week—Now What?

In Step 5, you made a plan for how to prepare for the different sections of the SAT exam. Now, you need a plan for how to approach test day. In the last week before the test, there are a few things you'll want to do in order to be ready for test day.

- **Continue to study every day or every other day, but don't cram.** The work you put in in the weeks and months prior to test day will make a big difference—not what you do in the last few days. Plan accordingly so that you don't feel pressured to stay up late or do anything extreme just before the test.

- **Pack your bag with the essentials.** The night before the test, or even earlier in the week, pack:

  ❑ your calculator with fresh batteries

  ❑ several sharpened non-mechanical #2 pencils

  ❑ your admission ticket

  ❑ some form of photo identification (a school ID is fine)

  ❑ a snack and water bottle for the break

  We also recommend wearing a watch—smartwatches are not permitted, but a digital watch is fine as long as you are certain it won't make noise during the test. Laying out your outfit the night before is also a good idea—one less thing to worry about in the morning.

- **Keep stress at bay.** The best way to avoid test anxiety is to be prepared. By fully preparing in the weeks leading up to the test, you'll help yourself feel more confident and less anxious on test day. If you do find yourself getting stressed out, take a break! Remember, this is just a test, and it's only one component of your college application. Make sure to take time for activities that you find relaxing. If you start to feel burned out on test prep, spend less time working on the SAT. Remember, what you do in the last week isn't as important as the work you have already put in.

- **Focus on areas of strength.** The last week before the test isn't the time to tackle the topics you find the most challenging. Build confidence by practicing your stronger areas—remember, playing to your strengths is key in improving your score.

- **Plan out your route.** If you'll be taking the test someplace other than your high school, it's a good idea to take a test drive to the location so that you know how to get there and how long it will take.

'Twas the Night Before the SAT...

The day before the test, stop studying! If 30 minutes of review would help you feel more confident, go for it, but don't do any more than that. The night before the test is your time to relax—whatever that means for you. Keep in mind this is not the time to binge watch a new TV show, go to a party, or play an addictive video game. After the SAT, you have our permission to reward yourself and spend the rest of the day on whatever you find the most fun. But on the night before the test, you don't want to do anything too stimulating or anything that will inadvertently cause you to stay up too late—you won't be able to get that time back. In fact, it's best to stay away from electronics for an hour or two before going to bed. Plan to go to bed about nine hours before you need to get up the next morning.

> If you tend to have trouble falling asleep the night before a big day, it can help if you've gotten a good night of sleep the night before that. That is, if your test is on a Saturday, make sure you go to bed early on Thursday—it will help you be a little more rested even if you don't sleep as well as you'd like on Friday night.

The Big Day

The day has finally arrived to put your SAT skills to the test—literally! Set your alarm early so that you have plenty of time in the morning. This is not the day to roll out of bed and stumble into the test center half asleep. It's a good idea to do 10 minutes of exercise (think jogging around the block or doing some push-ups) and/or take a shower to help yourself fully wake up and get blood and oxygen flowing to your brain. Eat a healthy breakfast (no doughnuts!), and eat a good amount—it's going to be about five or six hours before you'll be able to eat lunch. Don't try anything you don't normally do: test day isn't a good time to see what happens if you have coffee or an energy drink. Dress comfortably in layers, as regardless of the temperature outside, the classroom could be warm or cold. Remember to bring your bag of supplies and leave early, allowing time to park if necessary or to potentially wait in a line of cars dropping off students.

We recommend leaving your cell phone at home or in your car if possible. While (completely turned off) phones are permitted at the SAT, bringing one is risky, as you could have your score canceled if it makes a noise or if you accidentally look at it.

Some Surprising Factors that Can Significantly Affect Your SAT Score

- How confident you feel

- Being too cold or too hot

- The amount of sleep you got

- Wearing uncomfortable clothes

- Being hungry or thirsty

- Whether you are in a good or bad mood

Make sure to consider these other factors in addition to your test preparation when you are getting ready for test day. You don't want to counteract all of the hard work you have put into studying by being hungry, cold, or tired, for example.

What to Expect From the Testing Center

Most likely you will be asked to check in and present your admission ticket in a general area filled with students. You may have to wait for a while, and then you will be directed to the room you have been assigned to test in. Your room will have a proctor, an adult from your community whose job it is to administer the SAT. Your experience with the proctor will vary: some proctors will take the time to read you every word of the directions, while others will speed through them. Some will walk around the room, while others will sit the entire time. Some will provide 5-minute warnings when a section is nearing its end, but others won't.

Don't count on the proctor to help you out: use your own watch to ensure that you are given the right amount of time and to keep track of how much time is remaining.

Give Me a Break!

You will be allowed a 10-minute break between the Reading Test and the Writing and Language Test, and a 5-minute break between the two Math sections. Take advantage of these opportunities to leave the testing room, move around, have your snack and drink, and give your brain a break. That way you can come back feeling refreshed and ready to tackle the next portion of the test.

You may be asked to complete an additional 20-minute section that could be on any SAT topic. The College Board uses this section to test new questions, so most likely those questions won't count toward your score; however, there is always a chance that one or more could count, so try your best just in case. You will get a 2-minute break before this section.

What Could Go Wrong?

If any testing irregularities occur, be sure to inform your proctor if necessary and let the College Board know immediately. These irregularities include anything that significantly affects your ability to take the test, like the power going out, the proctor giving you the wrong amount of time or not following instructions, or students around you cheating. Of course, you should let your proctor know right away about anything that can be easily fixed (such as asking another student to stop tapping a pencil).

The Most Important Thing on Test Day

The SAT is a standardized test: that means it's roughly the same every time. By the time you take the test, you will have gotten very familiar with the SAT's structure and content, and you'll have learned strategies for the types of questions you can expect to see. Therefore, the most important thing you can do on test day is **stick to the plan**. Don't panic and go back to how you might have approached the SAT prior to prepping for it. Remember that you are well prepared, and execute the plan you have made for how to approach the test.

It's so important, we're going to say it again: *stick to the plan on test day*. If you've prepared, there shouldn't be any surprises—the test should be just as you're expecting.

...Now What?

In most cases, you should receive your SAT scores online about two weeks after taking the test. If, when you registered for the test, you chose to send your scores to colleges, those scores will be sent automatically. If you wish to send your scores to additional schools (or you didn't initially choose to send them), you can do that for a small fee at any time after receiving your score report.

Sending SAT Scores to Colleges

There are two ways to send your SAT scores.

1. As we discussed earlier, one way is to enter the names of up to four colleges when you register for the test. If you will be sending college applications within a few months, you can use this option. The benefit is that these score reports are free to you; the downside is that you'll have to select this option prior to seeing your scores. Even if you're not happy with your scores, they'll be sent anyway.

2. If you're not applying to colleges yet or you'd like to see your scores first, you can choose to send your score report(s) later. The drawback is you'll have to pay for each one; however, if you end up taking the SAT more than once, you'll be able to choose which test date(s) you wish to send. If you take the SAT three times, for example, you could choose to send all three sets of scores, just one date that has the highest overall score, or the two best dates. Remember, some schools require you to send the scores from all dates on which you took the test, while others require you to send only one date. As we discussed in Step 1, you must do your research to see what each school requires you to send.

You Made It!

Congratulations! You've found your best-fit colleges, learned how to improve your score, and successfully conquered the SAT. Reward yourself for that accomplishment and wait for the college acceptance letters to come in. Even though you may never have to use some of your SAT skills again (hopefully!), we encourage you to employ the self-confidence you've gained from mastering this test to succeed in your next chapter: higher education at the school of your choice. Now if you can just figure out what you want to major in…

NOTES

NOTES

NOTES

NOTES

NOTES

NOTES